I0423763

The Devastation and Economics of the African Holocaust

Dwayne Wong (Omowale)

Copyright © 2016 Dwayne Wong (Omowale)

All rights reserved.

ISBN: 1533510873
ISBN-13: 978-1533510877

CONTENTS

1 INTRODUCTION

"We do not desire what has belonged to others, though others have always sought to deprive us of that which belonged to us."
-Marcus Garvey

Prior to Christopher Columbus' arrival in the New World, Africa had produced a number of thriving civilizations. Some of which included Ghana, Mali, Songhai, Kanem-Bornu, Bushongo, Kush, and Axum. Europe, on the other hand, was in a much different situation. After the fall of the Western Roman Empire in 476, Western Europe experienced a period of decline and stagnation. The Eastern Roman Empire or Byzantine Empire survived until 1453 when it was conquered by the Turks. As the Catholic Church was preoccupied with the threat of the Turks in the eastern part of Europe, Western Europe had to deal with the threat of the Moors.

In 1492, Spain was now emerging from more than 700 years of Moorish domination. In 711 a general named Tariq ibn Ziyad sailed to Spain with his troops where they assisted the Visigoths in their rebellion against King Roderic in Spain. In the ensuing battle Roderic was killed, laying the basis for Musa ibn Nusair to bring his armies into Spain. The Moors eventually conquered the nation. The Moorish conquest in Europe was halted by the Franks led by Charles Martel at the Battle of Tours in 732. This victory prevented Moorish domination from spreading throughout Europe, but the centuries of Moorish domination in Iberia would have a

1

lasting impact on Europe's development.

Spain finally rid itself of Moorish rule in 1492 under the leadership of Ferdinand II and Isabella, royal cousins who were married in 1469. With the establishment of Catholic rule in Spain also came a quest to rid the nation of other religious influences. Muslims in Spain were given the choice of either voluntary exile or conversion to Christianity. Jews faced the same situation.

1492 was also the year that Christopher Columbus would fundamentally alter the destiny of Europe and of Africa. Using the funding that was provided to him by Ferdinand II and Isabella, Columbus sailed to the Americas. Columbus was attempting to sail to Asia, but he landed in the Caribbean instead. From the onset Columbus' intentions were the subjugation of the native population. In his journal Columbus notes: "They neither carry nor know anything of arms, for I showed them swords, and they took them by the blade and cut themselves through ignorance." Columbus also concluded that "with fifty men they can all be subjugated and made to do what is required of them." This is precisely what would happen.

Columbus' discovery of the Americas led to a scramble on the part of the Europeans to colonize this New World. In 1494, Spain and Portugal signed the Treaty of Tordesillas, which divided the newly discovered territories between Spain and Portugal. This ordeal also demonstrated the typically arrogant manner in which the ruling elite in Europe set about conquering the world. This pope, who had never stepped foot in the Americas, was deciding the fates of all those who lived in the "New World." The same is also true for the monarchs of Europe. European monarchs ruled in Europe, but they had control over matters that took place in faraway colonies that they had never even physically been to. The Napoleonic Wars in Europe forced the Portuguese monarchy into exile in Brazil. This marked the first time that a European monarch set foot in one of their American colonies and the only time that the capital of a European empire was located outside of Europe. The relocation of the monarchy in Brazil would also lead to a series of events that culminated in Brazil gaining its independence from Portugal.

Another indicator of this arrogance was the practice of renaming territories that already had people living there. Columbus called the island he landed in "New Hispaniola." The entire region was renamed America after Amerigo Vespucci. The English territories in North America were known as New England, with some of these colonies being given names such as New York or New Jersey. The people that the Europeans subjected were too renamed, as indicated by the practice of renaming of enslaved Africans with European names.

The Spanish and Portuguese were the first to colonize the Americas, followed by others such as the Danish, the Dutch, the English, and the French. The Europeans engaged in a number of wars and conflicts between each other for control of territory in the Americas. The Portuguese settled in Brazil, where they fought the French and Dutch for control over the territory. The Dutch, especially, proved to be a challenge to Portugal's attempts at establishing dominance in Brazil. The Dutch managed to capture Pernambuco in 1630 and established Dutch Brazil, which lasted until 1654. Some of the most notable conflicts over American territory were fought in North America. These conflicts, known as the French and Indian Wars, were a series of wars that were fought between the British colonists and the French colonists for control. Native Americans also fought on both sides of the final conflict between Britain and France.

The American Revolutionary War also played into the larger European struggle over the Americas. The revolution of thirteen British colonies in North America provided an opportunity for France to avenge their territorial losses against the British during the previously mentioned wars between France and Britain. To this end, France provided support for the American colonies. A French general known as Lafayette also assisted America during the war. The war was concluded in 1783 and the United States of America had successfully achieved its independence.

Aside from the warfare to establish domination of territory in the Americas, there was also the matter of economically exploiting the resources of the Americas. This was often achieved through the usage of slave labor. The first victims of European slavery in the New World were not Africans. Prior to Africans being enslaved, the natives and Europeans were used as slave labor. The treatment of Native Americans was especially horrendous. In *A Brief Account of the Destruction of the Indies*, Bartolomé de las Casas gives the following description of atrocities that the Spanish inflicted in the Caribbean:

> In the Year 1509, the *Spaniards* sailed to the Islands of St. *John* and *Jamaica* (resembling Gardensa and Bee-hives) with the same purpose and design they proposed to themselves in the Isle of *Hispaniola,* perpetrating innumerable Robberies and Villanies as before; whereunto they added unheard of Cruelties by Murdering, Burning, Roasting, and Exposing Men to be torn to pieces by Dogs; and Finally by afflicting and harassing them with un-exampled Oppressions and torments in the Mines, they spoiled and unpeopled this Contrey of these Innocents. These two Isles containing six hundred thousand at least, though at this day there are scarce two hundred men to be found in either of them, the remainder perishing without the knowledge of Christian Faith or Sacrament.

In the United States, the native population underwent similar treatment. There were frequent wars over the lands of the native people. In 1830, Congress passed the Indian Removal Act, which was an act that authorized the removal of the native people from their homeland. This led to a forced relocation known as the Trail of Tears, in which it is estimated that thousands of the relocated natives died en route to their destinations. European settlers in North America also used biological warfare to wipe out the natives. During the rebellion of an Odawa chief named Pontiac, the Europeans gave the natives smallpox infected blankets.

In the case of the Northwest Indian War, which began in 1785 and lasted ten years, the natives became proxies for the British to undermine America. Although the Northwest territory was ceded to America, Britain maintained forts there and continued to support the natives, who were resisting American attempts to take control of the territory. After a series of defeats, President George Washington sent Anthony Wayne to lead an expedition in the war. This proved to be a success. America defeated the Western Confederacy of native tribes. This was the first of many territorial conflicts between the native people and the American government. The War of 1812 was yet another conflict between the United

States and Britain in which natives fought on both sides of the conflict.

The Native Americans were virtually wiped out in many locations in the Americas due to being overworked, diseases, war, and forced relocation. In the Caribbean the Europeans replaced Native American labor with that of Europeans. These European workers were indentured laborers, while others were convicts who were forced to labor as punishment. Others, such as the Irish, went to the Americas to escape the harsh oppression of feudalism in Europe. The harsh laws of feudal Europe punished a number of different offenses through execution. In 1667, there was a petition which requested that a wife who was convicted for theft to be transported to the West Indies rather than face the death penalty for her crime. Transportation eventually became a punishment for certain offenses, such as trade union activity.

The usage of European labor also had limitations. One of which was that Europe's decision to dump their unwanted population in their colonies was an unpopular one. Benjamin Franklin had criticized the "dumping upon the New World of the outcasts of the Old." Aside from the complaints of those who did not like the "dumping" of criminals on the New World, African slave labor proved to be more efficient. The governor of Barbados expressed this when he stated that "three blacks work better and cheaper than one white man."

African labor quickly overtook the labor of Europeans. The circumstances that European laborers endured were often harsh and whippings were a common punishment, but the European laborer was only in servitude for a limited period of time. Moreover, their children were born free. Such liberties were not awarded to Africans, who were treated much worse. There was also a racial element added to the enslavement of Africans, as white slave masters justified their oppression of Africans based on the assumed inferiority of Africans. Africans proved to be better equipped to withstand the labor than the natives were. One planter stated that "permission be given to bring Negroes, a race robust for labor, instead of natives, so weak that they can only be employed in tasks requiring little endurance, such as taking care of maize fields or farms." African labor also proved to be cheaper than the usage of laborers from Europe.

As mentioned before, one of the justifications for the enslavement of Africans was the idea that Africans were inferior. Another justification was that Africans were heathens that needed to be converted to Christianity for the sake of saving their souls. In his work *On the Equality of Human Races*, Haitian scholar Anténor Firmin explained:

> To carry out the salvation of their souls, these men were taken from their primitive homes, from the love of their families, without any concern for their physical and moral sufferings, and thrown into a ship which was suitable for the infamous traffic!

Turning once more to Firmin, he gives us the following imagery of the experience of enslaved Africans on the plantations:

> Imagine the slave thrown like some degraded merchandize to foreign and distant shores; stupefied and broken before he touched this earth where everything is unknown to him; beaten and bent under the load, malnourished, and working tirelessly […].

The enslavement, colonization, and oppression of African people are referred to in this work as the African Holocaust. The exact number of those killed in this holocaust is impossible to calculate, although some numbers will be given throughout this work. In *The Negro*, for instance, historian W.E.B. Du Bois suggested that as many as 100 million Africans were killed as the result of the slave trade. In the Congo Free State, it is estimated that as many as 10 million Africans were killed by the Belgians. These numbers also do not factor in those killed by racial violence in the United States after slavery was abolished, those killed in the colonial wars of conquest and the anti-colonial wars in Africa, those killed in neo-colonial conflicts in Africa, or those that died as a result of the state of poverty and underdevelopment that Africans have been living in as a result of the holocaust.

What makes the injustices that Africans suffered at the hands of Europeans all the more tragic was that Africans were completely unprepared for the onslaught that the Europeans were to bring with them. In most cases, the Europeans were given a warm and hospitable welcome by the African population. As was demonstrated by Columbus' writings, the Europeans often arrived at a particular location with the intent to conquer and enslave the local population already firmly entrenched in their minds. Many of the Native Americans did not recognize these intentions until it was too late, and this was also the case with Africans.

One example of the differing mentalities of Africans and Europeans was when an African chief named Mojimba sent a party out to welcome the European traveler Henry Stanley. Mojimba had heard from the drums that "a man with white flesh" was traveling down the Lulaba River. Mojimba assumed that this strange white man was one of their brothers that had drowned in the river and was returning back home. Mojimba and his people prepared a feast for the mysterious white man and put on their ceremonial clothing. They then sailed out in their canoes to meet Stanley, but they were greeted by gun fire. They retreated back to their village, where the white men followed. Mojimba and his people fled into the forest as the white visitors looted and burned the village, killing many villagers in the process. Mojimba complained:

> You call us wicked men, but you white men are much more wicked! You think because you have guns you can take away our land and our possessions. You have sickness in your heads, for that is not justice.

Based on Stanley's account of the incident, his men saw Mojimba's men chanting and shaking their spears in their canoes. Stanley mistook Mojimba's canoes for war canoes and ordered his men to open fire. As Mojimba's people retreated, Stanley had his men follow them into their villages where they continued the fighting. The conflict between Mojimba and Stanley was in many ways a representation of African and European relations during their initial meetings. Africans gave Europeans a warm and hospital welcome, and Europeans returned this hospitality with violence.

The relationship between Africans and Europeans is largely the history of domination and violence. Ngũgĩ wa Thiong'o writes that

Sir Frederick Hodgson demanding the Golden Stool of the Asante people and Cecil Rhodes demanding to be buried at the sacred burial sites of the kings of Matabele/Ndebele "were acts of triumph and humiliation." He continues on to explain:

> But the beheading of King Hintsa and the burial of Waiyaki alive, body up- side down, and the removal of the genitalia of the Africans in America, go beyond particular acts of conquest and humiliation: They are enactments of the central character of colonial practice in general and of Europe's contact with Africa in particular since the beginnings of capitalist modernity and bourgeois ascendancy. This contact is characterized by dismemberment. An act of absolute social engineering, the continent's dismemberment was simultaneously the foundation, fuel, and consequence of Europe's capitalist modernity.

At the end of this period of slavery and colonial domination— which can be marked from the first major slave raid in 1444 to the end of apartheid in 1994—Western nations were wealthy and prosperous, whereas African people were left in a state of underdevelopment, poverty, and misery. This oppression, this holocaust, has left African people in a state of perpetual suffering which continues to linger even after African nations have received their independence. As will be demonstrated in this work, Western nations have also continued to exploit African nations after independence. This neo-colonial situation has continued the process of Western nations profiting from the exploitation of African people.

Given the horrendous manner in which Africans were exploited, there have been a number of attempts to receive reparations or some form of compensation for African people, both in the Americas and in various parts of Africa. For instance, Namibia has sought reparations from Germany for the Namibian genocide; a genocide which shall be discussed in this work. There have also been a number of advocates of reparations for the descendants of enslaved Africans in the Americas and the Caribbean. Throughout this work it will be demonstrated that the oppression of African people at the hands of European nations did in fact have profound economic consequences, so that the notion of reparations for

African people cannot be merely dismissed as is sometimes done. Japanese who were victimized in America by being forced into internment camps or the Jewish victims of the holocaust in Germany provide two examples of an oppressed people that were given reparations, so the historical precedence for reparations is certainly there.

The purpose of this work is to provide a general overview of how Western nations enriched themselves through the suffering of African people, as well as to assess the toll that such exploitation took on African people from both an economic and humanitarian standpoint. The goal is to provide a general overview of both the devastation and the economics of the African Holocaust.

2 THE PROFITS OF SLAVERY

The Dutch brought a shipment of about 20 enslaved Africans to North America in 1619, which would begin the practice of African slavery in North America which would last until 1865. Prior to this, however, slavery was already being practiced in South America and in the Caribbean islands. In total, the institution of the slave trade and slavery in the Americas lasted over 400 years, and had a marked impact on both European and African societies. The slave trade helped to create the rise of the imperial European nations, while at the same time devastating African society and dehumanizing millions of African people.

Before even arriving on the slave plantations Africans were viewed as and reduced to being mere commodities. The slave traders cared little for the comfort of the slaves while transporting them. The slaves had to endure inhumane conditions on the way to the New World. The slaves were packed together like "rows of books on shelves." There was hardly any space for them to stand erect. With so many bodies packed closely together the heat was unbearable and the air reeked of excrement. Many slaves did not even survive the Middle Passage. Those who died onboard the slave ship were simply thrown overboard; discarded like cheap cargo.

If a slave was thrown overboard the slave traders could seek compensation from the insurers. This fact is apparent in the *Zong* incident. *Zong* was a slave ship that was owned by a Liverpool slave trading company. During one particular journey from West

Africa to Jamaica, many of the slaves onboard became ill and died. They lost 60 of their total group of 470 Africans. The ship lost almost half of its crew to sickness as well. The captain decided to throw all the sick slaves overboard so that they could claim the insurance on them. More than 130 Africans were thrown overboard. The owners of the *Zong* won compensation for their losses, although the decision was later overturned on appeal.

Once Africans arrived in the Americas they were sold on the auction blocks. Richard Ligon of Barbados described the process as thus: "When they are brought to us, the Planters put them out of the Ship, where they find them stark naked, and therefore cannot be deceived in any outward infirmity. They choose them, as they do Horses in a Market; the strongest, youthfullest, and most beautiful, yield the greatest prices." Stephanie Smallwood explains:

> So important was the appearance of physical vitality that oil of one kind or another was used to give captives' skin a superficial luster and mask the depletion, weakness, and exhaustion that would otherwise have been evident.

Smallwood also notes that such practices "could not completely conceal the truth." Buyers were disappointed to find that many of the slaves that they bought were in poor condition. In some cases the Africans that arrived were in such bad physical condition that there simply was no disguising it. On July 1, 1680, the *Coaster* arrived in Barbados. Onboard the ship was 214 captives, 34 of which died during the month long voyage. When they arrived in Barbados, some of them had swollen bodies. In 1681, the *Supply* landed in Nevis with a supply of 235 captives that were purchased at Calabar in West Africa. Only 59 survived the journey.

The economic benefits of the slave trade for Europe and the Americas were numerous. Many investment banks made profits from the slave trade. This included Barclay's Bank. David and Alexander Barclay were involved in the slave trade in 1756 and eventually married into banking families, which resulted in the creation of Barclay's Bank. The Heywood Bank was founded in 1773 and lasted until 1883 when it was bought by the Bank of Liverpool. The founders of the Heywood Bank were merchants that were involved in the African trade. Thomas Leyland made his fortunes through the slave trade and then teamed up with Bullins to form the Leyland and Bullins bank. In 2005, J.P. Morgan admitted that between 1831 and 1865, two of its predecessor banks used more than 10,000 slaves as loan collateral. When borrowers defaulted on these loans the bank took ownership of these slaves.

In the United States, New England states such as Massachusetts, Rhode Island, and Connecticut were engaged in the slave trade. Of the New England involvement in the trade Thomas Pemberton wrote "that a large trade to Guinea was carried on for many years by the citizens of Massachusetts Colony, who were the proprietors of the vessels and their cargoes, out and home. Some of the slaves purchased in Guinea, and I suppose the greatest part of them, were sold in the West Indies." From the West Indies, slave traders brought back molasses which was used to make rum in New England. Therefore, the rum-distilling industry in New England was founded largely on the trade of Africans.

The slave trade also helped to finance industrial innovations. It was money acquired from the West Indian slave trade that helped to finance James Watt's steam engine. Antony Bacon, the 18th century iron monger, earned money from slavery prior to establishing his iron works business. Bacon also had a partnership with Gilbert Francklyn, who was a slave planter. Francklyn was a strong advocate of Britain taking over the French colony of Saint Domingue (later known as Haiti). In North America, slavery was an important aspect of the building of railroads. Norfolk Southern, CSX Transportation, and Canadian National all owned railroad lines that were built by slaves. The report on this story by *USA Today* notes:

> The president of Union Pacific's Memphis, El Paso & Pacific Railroad wrote to stockholders in 1858 that slaves were the "cheapest, and in the main most reliable, most easily governed" laborers.

Slavery in Brazil played a major role in the development of Portugal. By the mid-sixteenth century, Portugal established a thriving sugar economy in Brazil. This would last until the seventeenth century when a number of setbacks caused a decline in the sugar monopoly held by the Portuguese and Dutch. Between 1580 and 1640, Portugal was incorporated into Spain, and Spain was at the time in war with Holland. As a result the Dutch were driven out of Brazil in 1654, taking their technical knowledge of sugar production with them. The Dutch turned their attention towards expanding sugar production in the Caribbean and ultimately Caribbean sugar overtook Brazilian sugar. With the discovery of gold in Brazil, there was a gold rush. The site with the largest concentration of gold was in Minas Gerais. Just like sugar production, the production of gold also required the use of slave labor. Many Africans were taken from the sugar fields and made to work in the gold mines.

Starting in about 1840, Brazil's economy again shifted, but this time towards coffee. The cultivation of coffee had a bigger impact on Brazil's economy than both sugar and gold did. Much of the reason for this is that Brazil had since gained independence from Portugal and was struggling financially. Much like sugar and gold, it was slave labor that played a major role in the cultivation of coffee. Subsequently, when the demand for Brazil to abolish slavery became greater and the number of slaves available for labor began to shrink, the coffee industry suffered as well. During the 1870s—which is the decade before Brazil would officially outlaw slavery—there was a labor shortage that had to be offset by bringing in immigrant labor.

For the French Empire the slave trade was so profitable that Bishop Maury argued against ending the slave trade in 1791, stating:

> If you were to lose each year more than 200 million livres that you now get from your colonies; if you had not the exclusive trade with your colonies to feed your manufactures, to maintain your navy, to keep your agriculture going, to repay for your imports, to provide for your luxury needs, to advantageously balance your trade with Europe and Asia, then I say it clearly, the kingdom would be irretrievably lost.

It is clear that the slave trade was very beneficial to Europeans in a number of different ways. Slavery was such a big business that the

British established the Royal African Company. The Royal African Company was a chartered company that had a monopoly on the British slave trade. Originally the British had the Company of Royal Adventurers Trading to Africa, but that company was not very successful and eventually collapsed. The difficulties that Company of Royal Adventurers Trading to Africa encountered were due mainly to a war with Holland.

The Dutch had established a similar company known as the Dutch West India Company in 1621, which was a merger of all the private companies that were engaged in the Trans-Atlantic slave trade. This company provided Africans mainly to Brazil, but also to the English plantations as well. The British were displeased by this and worked to wrestle control of the slave trade away from the Dutch. Following two wars between the British and the Dutch, Britain emerged as the number one slave trading nation in Europe. The British also seized control of New Netherland, which were Dutch colonies in North America.

In 1713, the British signed the Assiento with the Spanish. This was a treaty that gave Britain a monopoly on supplying Spanish colonies with slaves. Britain seized on this opportunity by eagerly supplying the Spanish colonies with an estimated 144,000 slaves. This treaty was ended in 1750 and shortly afterwards the Royal African Company went bankrupt.

British politicians benefited from the slave trade. Former British Prime Minister William Ewart Gladstone was the son of Sir John Gladstone. John Gladstone had amassed his wealth from the West Indian slave trade. This fact did not go unnoticed while William Gladstone was campaigning. A public journal noted that he was "the son of Gladstone of Liverpool, a person who had amassed a large fortune by West India dealings. In other words, a great part of his gold has sprung from the blood of black slaves." This fact did not prevent Gladstone from becoming elected, however. Various United States presidents were also slave owners. The list of slave owning presidents includes: George Washington, Thomas Jefferson, James Madison, James Monroe, Andrew Jackson, James Polk, and Zachary Taylor.

The use of African slave labor was an essential part of the development of the New World. Enslaved Africans were described as "the strength and sinews of this western world." It was such an essential part of the development of the western world that the abolishment of slavery was a gradual process. The slave trade was such a profitable business for those living in the United States that the following report explains:

> The number of persons engaged in the slave-trade, and the amount of capital embarked in it, exceed our powers of calculation. The city of New York has been until of late [1862] the principal port of the world for this infamous commerce; although the cities of Portland and Boston are only second to her in that distinction. Slave dealers added largely to the wealth of our commercial metropolis; they contributed liberally to the treasuries of political organizations, and their bank accounts were largely depleted to carry elections in New Jersey, Pennsylvania, and Connecticut.

Keep in mind that during the time period that the above passage is referencing, slavery had been abolished throughout the northern states and the slave trade had been made illegal. Despite this, the importation of enslaved people from Africa remained a profitable business for northern states. In a span of eighteen months during 1859 and 1860, eighty-five slave ships are reported to have sailed out of the New York harbor. Even a British consul reported: "Almost all the slave expeditions for some time past have been fitted out in the United States, chiefly at New York."

The abolition of slavery was a gradual process and one often filled with hypocrisy on the part of the many of the abolitionists. Early in the nineteenth century European nations began gradually abolishing the slave trade. In 1792, Denmark passed a decree which declared an end to the slave trade in 1803. France abolished the slave trade in 1794 temporarily before restoring it again in 1799. Napoleon finally abolished the slave trade in 1815. The Netherlands abolished the slave trade in 1814. Brazil was the last nation to outlaw the slave trade, doing so in 1850 after intense pressure from the British. The United States, in particular, had made numerous attempts to abolish the slave trade, but none of these attempts were carried out wholeheartedly. The American constitution had stipulated that no laws prohibiting the slave trade were to be passed prior to 1807. Article 1, Section 9 reads:

> The Migration or Importation of such Persons as any of the States now existing shall think proper to admit, shall not be prohibited by the Congress prior to the Year one thousand eight hundred and eight, but a tax or duty may be imposed on such Importation, not exceeding ten dollars for each Person.

There were still a large number of slaves being imported into the United States between 1807 and 1865, despite the fact that in 1807 Thomas Jefferson passed the Act Prohibiting Importation of Slaves. Due to the stipulation laid out in the Constitution, Jefferson's act did not take effect until 1808. Though the act was passed, America enforced it poorly and the importation of slaves from Africa still continued. Prior to the 1807 Act, there was the Slave Act of 1794 which also sought to limit American involvement in the slave trade. The law was meant to "to prohibit the carrying on the Slave Trade from the United States to any foreign place or country," but this act was poorly enforced. Another bill passed in 1803, in response to the revolution that was raging in Haiti, stipulated that any ship that brought "any negro, mulatto, or other person of color" into the United States had to be forfeited. This law was passed largely due to the concern over a number of freed Africans that were arriving in the United States from Guadeloupe.

It should also be pointed out that Jefferson's 1807 act did not end slavery itself. Jefferson himself continued to own slaves until his death. The purpose of the act was solely to end the importation of African slaves into America. In 1807, the British passed the Slave Trade Act, which was to accomplish the same goal of ending the trade in African slaves. Neither act truly stopped the slave trade, however. Slave traders found ways to get around the laws, including flying certain flags. As the following report notes:

> Notwithstanding the prohibitory act of America, which was passed in 1807, ships bearing the American flag continued to trade for slaves until 1809, when, in consequence of a

decision in the English prize appeal courts, which rendered American slave ships liable to capture and condemnation, that flag suddenly disappeared from the coast. Its place was almost instantaneously supplied by the Spanish flag, which, with one or two exceptions, was now seen for the first time on the African coast, engaged in covering the slave trade.

The laws regarding the inspection of slave ships were so sloppy that Lord John Russell commented: "It is ascertained, by repeated instances, that the practice is for vessels to sail under the American flag. If the flag is rightly assumed, and the papers correct, no British cruiser can touch them. If no slaves are on board, even though the equipment, the fittings, the water-casks, and other circumstances prove that the ship is on a Slave Trade venture, no American cruiser can touch them."

Robert Campbell, who was born in Jamaica, journeyed throughout Africa and eventually relocated to Lagos. In Sierra Leone he recalled seeing a slaver and he explained that one of the reasons why it was so difficult to suppress the slave trade was the light punishments that slavers received:

At Freetown, Sierra Leone, we saw a large slaver, brought in a few days before by H. M. S. S. "Triton." Her officers and crew, consisting of over thirty persons, were there set at liberty, to be disposed of by the Spanish Consul as distressed seamen. They were as such forwarded in the same ship with us to Teneriffe. No wonder that the slave-trade should be so difficult to suppress, when no punishment awaits such wretches as these. What scamp would fear to embark in such an enterprise, if only assured that there was no personal risk— that he has only to destroy the ship's flag and papers on the approach of a cruiser, not only to shield himself and his crew from the consequence of his crime, but to receive the consideration rightly accorded distressed honest men. These villains, of course return to Havana or the United States, procure a new ship, and again pursue the wicked purpose which their previous experience enables them to accomplish with all the more impunity.

In 1818, the United States passed a new act regarding the importation of slaves to fix the faults of the 1807 act. This act was poorly constructed and did not effectively address the problem. Another bill was passed in 1819. This bill allowed the president to use armed cruisers on the coasts of the United States and Africa to suppress the slave trade. Under this law, the captors of these ships were also provided with a bounty.

Despite the efforts taken to abolish and restrict the slave trade, the slave trade still continued and large numbers of slaves were taken from Africa. The slave trade was one of the topics discussed at the Congress of Verona in 1822. This congress was attended by Austria, France, Britain, Russia, and Prussia. At the meeting the British delegates complained that the slave trade had actually increased in volume, despite the fact that only Portugal and Brazil still allowed the trade. The British delegates recommended three proposals to prevent the slave trade, but none of these proposals were accepted.

W.E.B. Du Bois gives the following description of the slave trade from 1820 until 1860:

> Estimates as to the extent of the slave-trade agree that the traffic to North and South America in 1820 was considerable, certainly not much less than 40,000 slaves annually. From that time to about 1825 it declined somewhat, but afterward increased enormously, so that by 1837 the American importation was estimated as high as 200,000 Negroes annually. The total abolition of the African trade by American countries then brought the traffic down to perhaps 30,000 in 1842. A large and rapid increase of illicit traffic followed; so that by 1847 the importation amounted to nearly 100,000 annually. One province of Brazil is said to have received 173,000 in the years 1846-1849. In the decade 1850-1860 this activity in slave-trading continued, and reached very large proportions.

Despite the abolition of the slave trade by most Western nations, there was no serious attempt to stem the trade in Africans. As Du Bois demonstrated, a large number of Africans were being imported into the Americas, especially in Brazil, after the abolition of the slave trade. Anne Bailey points out that during the abolition of the slave trade there was actually an increase in the importation of slaves:

> Abolition in 1807 did little to deter slave traders, and, in fact, in the 1820s and 1830s, there was an unprecedented increase in the traffic. It is estimated that more slaves crossed the Atlantic at that time than at any other period in history.

Much of this was due to the fact that the abolition of the slave trade (as well as slavery) was not completely driven by sympathy. Du Bois explained that "philanthropy was not working alone to overthrow Negro slavery and the slave trade. It was seen, first in England and later in other countries, that slavery as an industrial system could not be made to work satisfactorily in modern times." In other words, as America moved towards industrialization, slave plantation labor became much less effective. For those in power the abolition of slavery meant moving towards a more effective means of production, and as such little sympathy was given to the Africans that continued to suffer even after the abolition of slavery. This also meant that there were no serious incentives for the ruling class to quickly abolish slavery, which is why America's constitution actually protected the slave trade for twenty years.

There was much resistance towards the end of slavery on the part of the planters. In the United States, differences between Northern and Southern states over the question of slavery resulted in a civil war. Whereas Northern states had, for the most part, abolished slavery, the South's economy still relied on slave labor. In Jamaica some planters considered secession from Britain over the issue of abolition.

There was also a great level of hypocrisy in the British abolition movement as they not only neglected slavery outside of the British colonies, but they continued to benefit from that same system of slavery. Eric Williams writes:

> The abolitionists were boycotting the slave-grown produce

of the British West Indies, dyed with the Negro's blood. But the very existence of British capitalism depended upon the slave- grown cotton of the United States, equally connected with slavery and polluted with blood. The West Indian could legitimately ask whether "slavery was only reprehensible in countries to which those members do not trade, and where their connections do not reside."

Williams further points out that the "boycotters of West Indian sugar sat upon chairs of Cuban mahogany, before desks of Brazilian rosewood, and used inkstands of slave-cut ebony […]." Therefore it was impossible for a nation like England to completely abstain from slave products, unless they were willing to "betake themselves to the woods and live on roots and berries." The British capitalists refused to give up Brazilian sugar and the abolitionists sided with them.

Of the abolitionist response to slavery in Cuba and Brazil, Williams describes:

> Brazilian and Cuban economy depended on the slave trade. Consistency alone demanded that the British abolitionists oppose this trade. But that would retard Brazilian and Cuban development and consequently hamper British trade. The desire for cheap sugar after 1833 overcame all abhorrence of slavery. Gone was the horror which once was excited at the idea of a British West Indian slave-driver armed with a whip; the Cuban slave-driver, armed with whip, cutlass, dagger and pistols, and followed by bloodhounds, aroused not even comment from the abolitionists.

In Haiti the enslaved Africans arose and freed themselves from the shackles of slavery. British Prime Minister William Pitt, himself an advocate of abolishing the slave trade, launched an effort to capture Haiti for Britain. This move was obviously motivated by the sugar production in Haiti, which was built on the backs of slave labor. William Wilberforce noted that "Pitt threw out against slave motion on St. Domingo account." Under Pitt not only did the

British slave trade increase, but so too did Britain's sugar empire. Guiana and Trinidad became British territories.

The end of slavery hardly meant the end of the exploitation of the newly freed Africans. Those in the British controlled Caribbean territories still found themselves living under British domination and the living conditions were harsh. This is summed up by a song from a singer named Patrick Jones, who sang in 1920:

> Britain boasts of democracy,
>
> Brotherly love and fraternity,
>
> But British colonists have been ruled in perpetual misery

In the British colony of Jamaica, the 1865 Morant Bay Rebellion best exemplifies how unsatisfied black people still were at their condition. Although slavery was over, the black population was still impoverished and discriminated against by the white minority on the island. Frustrated with their current situation and by the lack of any meaningful attempts to change things, many of the blacks rebelled. Leading this rebellion was Paul Bogle. Governor Edward John Eyre decided to brutally crush the rebellion. Bogle was later captured and hanged. George William Gordon, a politician and critic of Eyre, was also captured and executed. Slavery was over in Jamaica, but black people were nevertheless still oppressed under British colonial rule, and this was not only the case in Jamaica, but also in the other British colonies in the Caribbean.

We can look at British Guiana as yet another example of the struggles that African people faced following independence. Despite the abolition of slavery, the plantation class remained in control, as Walter Rodney explained:

> In Guiana, planters who had invested in polders, land, slaves, and machinery were not defeated and crushed locally by the slave masses. They remained firmly in control of the post-Emancipation legislature and were confirmed in the ownership of all property except the slaves.

Given these realities, the newly freed Africans found themselves once again at odds with the plantation owners. Among the issues that emerged was that the African population wanted higher wages and more independence than the estate owners were willing to give them. The clash between the two resulted in sugar strikes in 1842 and 1848. The departure of Africans from the sugar plantations led to a shortage in labor, which is something that some in the Caribbean had warned against. In Trinidad, Lord Howick, who worked as the Under Secretary of State for the Colonies, recognized as early as 1832 that emancipation would bring forth a problem in which Africans cease working on sugar plantations: "The great problem to be solved in drawing up any plan for the emancipation of the Slaves in our Colonies, is to devise some mode of inducing them when relieved from the fear of the Driver and his whip, to undergo the regular and continuous labour which is indispensable in carrying on the production of Sugar."

In British Guiana, Indians came to make up the largest number of those who were imported to replace African slave labor, although indentured laborers were also brought from China and the island of Madeira in Portugal. Therefore, after abolishing slavery, the British in Guiana simply exploited the labor of other oppressed groups. Indians were also brought to Trinidad and other Caribbean territories as well. The introduction of Indian labor also had the effect of undermining the struggles of Africans for better wages. Walter Rodney explains:

> In British Guiana, as in Trinidad, Martinique, and Jamaica, the principal objection made by African descendants to the waves of indentured Indians was that they were a threat to employment. In 1846-47, indentured immigrants were unwitting strikebreakers on the Guianese sugar estates; and in Creole eyes, this image was retained for a long while.

After slavery was abolished in the Caribbean, Africans found themselves in a position where they were being forced to work for small wages. This was the case in Guiana, where Rodney notes:

> On the termination of apprenticeship on 1 August 1838,

workers demanded more than employers were prepared to pay and they began exercising a greater degree of independence than the estates would tolerate. The struggle that resulted, and that assumed the form of protracted sugar strikes in 1842 and 1848, strengthened the determination of planters to secure immigrant laborers whose conditions of indenture service excluded the right to seek out new employers and whose wage rates were also statutorily restricted.

As they did with Africans who were used as slave labor, the Europeans also came to view Indians as being an inferior people who were fit for servitude. Lord Harris, the Governor of Trinidad, declared of both Africans and Indians: "The only independence which they would desire is idleness, according to their different tastes in the enjoyment of it; and the higher motives which actuate the European labourer […]." Given the negative views of Indians, it is not surprising that the Indian laborers were treated very harshly by the plantation system. From 1909 to 1912, there were nearly 8,000 cases of Indians in Trinidad being prosecuted. The main offense that was committed was desertion. Other offenses included being absent from work without a lawful excuse or not finishing work. Vagrancy was a crime that was punishable by the law. Laws concerning Indians restricted their freedom of movement and ensured that they remained on the plantations.

The wages that the Indians received was a mere pittance of the massive amount of the wealth that the plantation managers received from Indian labor. In British Guiana, in 1912, the average weekly earnings of an indentured laborer were $1.23 in Demerara and Berbice. It was slightly less in Essequibo, being $1.14. Indians also had to endure terrible living conditions on the plantations. A memorandum that was submitted by Mr. Lechmere Guppy to the Royal Franchise Commission of 1888 exposed what living conditions were like for Indians in Trinidad:

As first in the list of evils which afflict the Colony, I look upon the system of housing the Indian Immigrants in barracks. It was not introduced until after Major Fagan had been dismissed and the subjugation of the coolie to a five

0# Dwayne Wong (Omowale)

years' indenture to a master imposed upon him by the Government had become complete. At the outset barracks were only built for the Indians who came unaccompanied by women, and free labourers were lodged as before in separate cottages. The first in Naparima was erected at Palmyra Estate, and I think that one was the first in the Island: but as the estates got fully supplied with coolies the cheapness of the barrack caused it to be adopted universally. The barrack is a long wooden building eleven or twelve feet wide, containing perhaps eight or ten small rooms divided from each other by wooden partitions not reaching to the roof. The roof is of galvanised iron, without any ceiling; and the heat of the sun by day and the cold by night take full effect upon the occupants. By standing on a box the occupant of one room can look over the partition into the adjoining one, and can easily climb over. A family has a single room in which to bring up their boys and girls if they have children. All noises and talking and smells pass through the open space from one end of the barrack to the other. There are no places for cooking, no latrines. The men and women, boys and girls, go together into the canes or bush when nature requires. Comfort, privacy and decency are impossible under such conditions. A number of these barracks are grouped together close to the dwelling house of the overseers, in order that they may with the least trouble put them out to work before daylight in crop time, which they do by entering their room and, if necessary, pulling them off their beds where they are lying with their wives. If a man is sick he is not allowed to be nursed by his wife, he must perforce go to the hospital far away, leaving his wife, perhaps without the means of subsistence, in such a room as I have described, to her own devices, amid the temptations surrounding her. With all this, can any one wonder at the frequent wife-murders and general demoralisation amongst the Indian immigrants? In fact the barrack life is one approaching to promiscuous intercourse. And the evil is not confined to the coolies. No decent black labourer can take his wife to live amongst such surroundings. For very long past I have watched the spread

24

of immorality among the lower classes consequent on the barrack system. At first the married negro who was employed in crop time on a plantation left his wife in San Fernando or other place where he had a cottage, returning to his home on Saturday night and leaving it again on Monday morning. Thus the husband and wife were parted for a week, and too often formed other relations. Mutual support and comfort existed no longer, the moral tie was broken and it was clear that marriage was a useless unmeaning clog which it is no shame to omit. From the estates the curse has spread to the towns. It is a more profitable investment to build barracks and let single rooms in them than to build detached cottages: and unmarried men and unmarried women occupy in this manner whole ranges of rooms. On plantations the demoralization is carried as far as it can go. The absentee proprietor is not there to witness the scandals. The overseers will tell you, as I have often been told by them, that they are put there to make sugar and not to look after the morals of coolies. The owner in England compares notes with other absentees and expects his crop to be made at the lowest rate. As to the means, that matters not to him. The overseer holds his situation subject to twenty-four or forty-eight hours' notice and to escape losing his place and consequent beggary he must have but one object in view: that of screwing the most he can out of his bondsman.

This lengthy quote above describes a situation of complete neglect on the part of the British administration in Trinidad. Conditions for Indians were little better in other Caribbean territories. The government of India investigated the conditions of Indian immigrants in Trinidad, as well as three other British colonies and Suriname in 1913. They found that the Indian population was infected with hookworm, malaria, and other illnesses. Given the living conditions described in the barracks in which Indians lived, such illnesses are not surprising. Treatment for such illnesses was also very poor as well. In British Guiana, it was often the case that doctors that were in charge of estate hospitals would certify that sick indentured laborers were fit for labor, even if that was not the case.

Not surprisingly, such deplorable situations often led to resistance on the part of the exploited Indians. Eric Williams points out that one tactic which was used by indentured Indians was to feint being sick to avoid work:

> [T]he indentured Indian immigrant resorted to the only weapon at his command - passive resistance. He simply malingered, or pretended to be sick, or went into the hospital. Some positively alarming statistics of the man-days lost in hospital are available for the West Indies. In French Guiana, in the first six months of 1875, where the indentured immigrants averaged 350 a month, the man-days worked numbered 26,852, and the man-days lost in hospital 26,602; the average number of days worked by each immigrant was twelve per month, while, for every day worked, one day was spent in the hospital. In Trinidad, in 1895, for 10,720 Indian immigrants, there were 23,688 admissions to hospitals. Thus each Indian went at least twice a year to the hospital, at the expense of the planter and the government.

Indian resistance in British Guiana was often very direct. Bechu, who arrived from Bengal and was indentured to Plantation Enmore in 1894, was unfit for heavy manual labor. Instead, he performed domestic tasks until his indentureship was finished in February 1897. By this time Bechu had since become an outspoken critic of the abuses of the indentureship system. In 1896 he wrote a letter to the press in which he spoke about the exploitation of Indian women at the hands of overseers and Indians being turned away from estate hospitals. Bechu's writings led to the dismissal of some overseers, but they also made Bechu a target of the planters. On two occasions Bechu was charged for libel.

Bechu wrote:

> My countrymen like myself have had the misfortune to come to Demerara, the political system of which colony has very appropriately been divined and defined by Mr.

Trollope under a happy inspiration as "despotism tempered by sugar." To these twin forces, the Immigration system is as sacred as the old system of slavery in former days, and for one in my humble position to have ventured to touch it with profane hands or to have dared to unveil it is considered on this side of the Atlantic to be a capital and inexpiable offence.

The harsh treatment of the Indians on the sugar plantations led to frequent riots and rebellions. These rebellions by the Indian population created an interesting contradiction. On one hand, the Indians were described as being docile, but they were also depicted as being violent. Such conflicting stereotypes helped to justify the planters' treatment of their labor. Indians were viewed as being docile enough to be subjugated as indentured laborers, but because of their perceived violent nature the planters often had to enact harsh laws to keep them in place. This created a situation in which, as Rodney explains, when Indians attempted to protest peacefully "they were backed into a position of frustration and violence." The state of the Indian indentured laborers in the Caribbean was a reflection of the poor treatment that colonial subjects endured in the British Caribbean after the abolition of slavery.

In the 1930s there were riots all throughout the British West Indies due to the poor conditions of the colonies. An investigation was undertaken by the Royal Commission, but the reports could not be published until after World War II because the reports would have made the British look scarcely better than the fascists that they were fighting against. One of the most notable incidents of unrest in the 1930s in the British Caribbean was the 1937 disturbances by followers of the Grenadian born Tubal Uriah Butler. Butler had planned to stage a sit-down strike on the oilfields. Butler was a former employee of the oilfields, who became a labor leader demanding better conditions for oil workers. Initially the strike was a peaceful one, until the police attempted to arrest Butler as he was giving a speech. The crowd attacked the police and Butler escaped. An officer named Corporal King was beaten so severely that he broke his leg. He then had oil poured on him and was burnt to death. This sparked unrest across the country. Butler managed to evade arrest, despite the $500 reward that was offered for his capture. Butler eventually came out of hiding and was arrested. The entire incident made Butler a national hero and demonstrated the discontent of the oil workers in Trinidad and Tobago.

Africans in the French West Indies did not fare much better, despite opting to remain overseas French territories rather than achieving political independence as many former British colonies did. Toussaint L'Ouverture had come to describe France as a "step-mother" where the people of Saint Domingue (later Haiti) were concerned, but the notion of France as a mother country has prevailed in many of the French speaking territories. This is interesting given that it was in the French speaking colonies that the ideology of Negritude developed. The founders of this ideology include Aimé Césaire of Martinique, Leon Damas of French Guiana, and Léopold Senghor of Senegal. Negritude was developed mainly as a cultural movement, with little emphasis on radical demands for political or economic self-determination for African people. This inability to break with France has had profound economic consequences for the French West Indies, which continued to be economically dependent on France.

In 1948, 100 years after slavery had been abolished in Martinique the local economy had not changed radically. The African population was still impoverished, working on sugar cane plantations owned by the white elites of the island. The situation was so miserable that in 1948 some of the Martiniquans murdered a sugar mill owner named Guy Fabrique. He was chased by a mob and hacked to death with machetes. Aware of the possibility of rioting on the island, the whites in Martinique had approached the American consul William H. Christensen. They requested American military assistance in the case of race riots on the island. It was under these conditions that arguments in favor of making Martinique an overseas department of France emerged.

Aimé Césaire was very vocal about French racism and colonialism, but rather than opting for complete independence from France, Césaire argued in favor of making the French Caribbean colonies overseas territories. This was referred to as the "departmentalization" of the colonies. Among the colonies included were Martinique, Guadeloupe, French Guiana, and Réunion. The result has been that these overseas territories have continued to be neglected by the "Mother Country." In 2009, France faced revolts in both Guadeloupe and Martinique. The protests began in Guadeloupe in response to low wages, a high cost of living, and feeling neglected by France. Some also resented that the wealth of the island was still mostly in the hands of the descendants of the colonists. The protests in Guadeloupe also spread to Martinique. In the wake of the global financial crisis, unemployment in both colonies was double that of France's unemployment. French Guiana also threatened to launch similar protests.

Africans in the United States also faced a number of hardships following the end of slavery. The South had lost the American Civil War in 1865, and slavery was subsequently abolished. Not satisfied with this, the former slave masters sought ways to continue to use African Americans as slave labor. This is where the 13th amendment came in. This amendment, which we are told freed the slaves, also left room for the continued legal enslavement of African Americans. Section 1 of that amendment reads:

> Neither slavery nor involuntary servitude, except as a punishment for crime whereof the party shall have been duly convicted, shall exist within the United States, or any place subject to their jurisdiction.

Although slavery in the United States was abolished, forced labor still continued in the South. The southern economy could not function without the labor of African Americans so they began renting black prisoners to be used for slave labor by companies. One victim of this new form of slavery was Green Cottenham. He was arrested and charged with vagrancy—not being able to prove that you were employed was a felony. Labor was the punishment for vagrancy. Cottenham was sold to a company and was forced to work in a coal mine. Cottenham later died, unable to withstand the brutal working conditions. Many others endured a similar fate. Such individuals were often seized from the roads as they were walking from one place to another.

To restrict the free movement of African Americans, the laws stated that no black person could legally change their job without the permission of their employer. African Americans were now in a situation which was essentially slavery. This system of forced labor continued for many decades after slavery was abolished. In 1942, in response to Japanese propaganda, President Franklin Roosevelt ordered that the Department of Justice address the continued slavery in the South. One of the cases that were addressed was that of Alfred Irving, who was held as a slave for many years by a family in Texas. This same family was later convicted and sent to prison. Although the government began stemming the practice of slavery, the provision of the 13th amendment that allowed slavery as a form of punishment was never overturned.

It has been demonstrated that the slave trade and slave labor contributed greatly to the development of the capitalistic European system. For Africans, on the other hand, the slave trade had a destructive impact. The sheer number of humans stolen due to the Middle Passage alone had an adverse impact on Africa. President Sékou Touré of Guinea described this when he stated: "The relation between the degree of destitution of peoples of Africa and the length and nature of the exploitation they had to endure is evident. Africa remains marked by the crimes of the slave-traders: up to now, her potentialities are restricted by under-population." John Newton, himself a former slave trader, wrote:

> I have not sufficient data to warrant calculation, but, I suppose, not less than one hundred thousand slaves are exported, annually, from all parts of Africa, and that more than one-half of these are exported in English bottoms.
>
> If but an equal number are killed in war, and if many of these wars are kindled by the incentive of selling their prisoners; what an annual accumulation of blood there must be, crying against the nations of Europe concerned in this trade, and particularly against our own!

W.E.B. Du Bois gave an even more stark description of the toll that the slave trade took on the population of Africa:

> The total number of slaves imported is not known. Dunbar estimates that nearly 900,000 came to America in the

sixteenth century, 2,750,000 in the seventeenth, 7,000,000 in the eighteenth, and over 4,000,000 in the nineteenth, perhaps 15,000,000 in all. Certainly it seems that at least 10,000,000 Negroes were expatriated. Probably every slave imported represented on the average five corpses in Africa or on the high seas. The American slave trade, therefore, meant the elimination of at least 60,000,000 Negroes from their fatherland. The Mohammedan slave trade meant the expatriation or forcible migration in Africa of nearly as many more. It would be conservative, then, to say that the slave trade cost Negro Africa 100,000,000 souls. And yet people ask to-day the cause of the stagnation of culture in that land since 1600!

Although Europeans were able to build entire industries and enrich themselves from the slave trade, Africans gained no such benefits from the slave trade. Certainly the slave trade did benefit some of the African ruling class that was involved in the trade, but it only benefited them individually. Lansiné Kaba explains that "most of the individuals who participated directly belonged to the old or new elite of their society and acted primarily in their own interests." Thus African societies as a whole did not benefit from the trade.

Some of those who benefitted from the slave trade also became victims of the slave trade themselves. In *Capitalism and Slavery*, Eric Williams mentions the case of a slave trader who accepted a slave captain's invitation to dinner. Williams explains that the slave trader got drunk and "awoke next morning to find his money gone and himself stripped, branded and enslaved with his own victims [...]." It was not uncommon to find cases in which slave traders were themselves captured and enslaved due to the trickery of the European slavers.

There is also another element to this that Walter Rodney points out when he explains that "majority of the imports were of the worst quality even as consumer goods—cheap gin, cheap gunpowder, pots and kettles full of holes, beads, and other assorted rubbish." The products that Africans received were of poor quality. This was a carefully crafted policy on the part of the Europeans, who were very selective with what they gave to Africans. In 1514,

Portugal passed a code of regulations. Among the things prohibited in this code was the sale of paper to Africans. Despite the ban on paper, European traders still found themselves selling paper. Paper was especially sought after by African Muslims. The Susus had an Islamic school in which the young would be made to memorize the Qur'an by writing down verses and reading them aloud.

The European traders were also wary about allowing guns to come into the possession of African people. The Portuguese, especially, feared weapons falling into the hands of both Africans and Portuguese traders—there was a fear that with weapons the latter could make themselves independent of the Portuguese crown. In Upper Guinea, the French sold guns and gunpowder to Africans. Labat was so distressed by this practice that he advocated that "this trade should be discouraged by stiff penalties because of the terrible consequences of teaching these barbarous people the use of firearms." The Portuguese also prohibited swords from being sold to Africans.

Guns were a major commodity in the slave trade, yet the quality of guns that were given to the Africans was inferior to that which the Europeans possessed. Africans also were not educated to produce these weapons themselves either. Most requests made by the Africans to learn certain skills that the Europeans had were rejected, and because Africans could not make their own guns, they had to rely on secondhand or inferior weapons. It was not in the benefit of the Europeans to either teach the Africans how to make guns or give them advanced guns. The Maxim Machine Gun, in particular, played a very important role in the conquest of southern Africa. Europeans certainly never would have let such a weapon fall into the hands of the Africans. There was a saying in Dahomey which went: "He who makes the powder wins the war." They recognized the importance of controlling the gun in warfare and it would later be European firearms that conquered Dahomey.

Various Africans made requests to learn the technical skills that the Europeans had. The Asante king, Opoku Ware, requested that the Europeans establish factories and distilleries in his territory, but he got no response. Emperor Lebna Dengel of Ethiopia examined European goods and wanted to learn the technical knowledge that the Europeans had. He sent requests to rulers such as Manuel I and John III of Portugal and even Pope Leo X, but all of these requests were ignored. The reality is that the development of Africa was never a concern for the European colonizers. They were simply looking to make a profit and it was not in their best interest to educate Africans to possess the same level of technical knowledge.

Finally, the slave trade altered and disrupted the entire social structure in Africa. Turning once more to Lansiné Kaba, he explained:

> The slave trade disrupted and bled Africa. It undermined the viability of many states by fostering the rise of predatory, militaristic regimes devoid of any legitimacy. The sole purpose of these tyrants, whose regimes were known in Senegal as *ceddo*, was to enslave others in order to satisfy their need for firearms and luxury goods.

John Coleman De Graft-Johnson explains of this era in African history:

> Tribes had to supply slaves or be sold as slaves themselves, for this indeed was the age of the gangster. Violence, brutality, and ferocity became the necessities of survival, for generosity and good neighbourliness had lost their meaning.

In further describing the chaos of this era, Graft-Johnson writes:

> The stockades of grinning skulls, the selling of one's own children as slaves, the unprecedented human sacrifices, were all the sequel to this grand finale, the rape of African culture and civilization. The African could not understand what he had done to the gods to merit such horrors and cruelties, and as such his attempts to propitiate them became more and more extreme.

The picture that emerges from the slave trade is an event that devastated African societies, not only in the toll that it took on the population in terms of deaths, but also in the fact that it altered the very social structure of those societies. Warfare became more

33

commonplace and much more brutal than the skirmishes that had taken place prior to the arrival of Europeans. It was during this period that we see the emergence of more militarized and warlike African kingdoms such as Dahomey and Asante, both of which were also noted for their practice of human sacrifice, as well as their extensive involvement in the slave trade.

Aside from the damaging impact that the slave trade had on Africa, there is also the matter of the brutalities that were inflicted on enslaved African people in the Americas. In 1845, a planter in Brazil admitted that "slaves are badly fed, worse clothed, and work so hard that their lives do not exceed six years." Olaudah Equiano, who was himself a slave, gave a firsthand account of the brutalities that were inflicted on African people in the Caribbean. In Montserrat he witnessed a man being staked to the ground and having his ears cut off "bit by bit" for having relations with a white prostitute. He noted that in St. Kitts it was common "for the slaves to be branded with the initial letters of their master's name; and a load of heavy iron hooks hung about their necks." Equiano continues to explain that "the most trifling occasions they were loaded with chains; and often instruments of torture were added. The iron muzzle, thumb-screws, &c. are so well known, as not to need a description, and were sometimes applied for the slightest faults. I have seen a negro beaten till some of his bones were broken, for even letting a pot boil over."

Frederick Douglass depicts similar horrors as he recounted his own experience of being a slave in the United States:

> I lived with Mr. Covey one year. During the first six months, of that year, scarce a week passed without his whipping me. I was seldom free from a sore back. My awkwardness was almost always his excuse for whipping me. We were worked fully up to the point of endurance. Long before day we were up, our horses fed, and by the first approach of day we were off to the field with our hoes and ploughing teams. Mr. Covey gave us enough to eat, but scarce time to eat it. We were often less than five minutes taking our meals.

Julia Floyd Smith explains that for the crime of physically

touching a white person, a slave could be subjected to "having his hands burned with a heated iron, his ears nailed to a post, or a certain number of lashes by the whip." Slaves were also harshly punished for leaving the plantation without permission. Charlotte Martin recalled that her eldest brother was whipped to death for this offense.

One of the most horrific and macabre examples of enslaved Africans being mistreated was the case of a woman slave owner named Delphine LaLaurie. Delphine's activities were uncovered when on April 10, 1834 one of the slaves started a fire in the kitchen. Neighbors rushed into the house and uncovered the slave quarters. The slave that started the fire had been chained in the kitchen. Others were found in much worse off situations. One slave, an old man, was also found chained. His head "bore the appearance of having been beaten until it was broken" and his brain was being devoured by worms. Another woman was whipped so badly on her back that the bones were exposed. Other beaten and bruised slaves were found throughout the house.

Slaves were frequently abused and tortured, and the law was always on the side of the slave masters. Slave masters were free to use violence against their property, but laws were harsh towards those slaves who fought back. In 1824, three years after the United States took Florida from Spain, a law was passed which decreed: "Be it further enacted that if any slave shall consult, advise, or conspire to rebel, or make insurrection against the white inhabitants of this territory, or against the laws of the government thereof, or shall plot or conspire the murder of any white person, or shall commit an assault and battery, on any white person with an intention to kill, he or she shall, on conviction of either of the said crimes, suffer death." It was also legal to kill runaway slaves. In one case, a slave owner named J.S. McDonnell placed a notice in which he offered a $150 reward for killing his three runaway slaves and $20 each for having them returned alive to his plantation. Such "dead or alive" rewards were not uncommon.

Given such harsh circumstances, it is not surprising that many slaves committed suicide to escape subjugation. It was not uncommon for slaves to throw themselves overboard on the slave ships whenever they got an opportunity. Olaudah Equiano described that one African was so miserable that he attempted to starve himself to death. This resulted in him being flogged. He then tried to jump overboard, but was rescued. Some Africans engaged in ritualistic suicide to escape their plight. The Cuban runaway slave Esteban Montejo recorded that slaves would tie a chain to their waists before throwing themselves into rivers. They believed that this chain was "full of magic." Many Africans committed suicide in hopes that they would return again to their homeland.

In writing of slavery in Brazil, Thomas Ewbank explained:

> Suicides continually occur, and owners wonder. The high-souled Minas, both men and women, are given to self-destruction. Rather than endure life on the terms it is offered, many of them end it. Then they that bought them grind their teeth and curse them, hurl imprecations after their flying spirits, and execrate the saints that let them go. If individuals are ever justified in using the power Heaven has placed in their hands to terminate at once their earthly existence, it must be these. Those who blame them for putting the only barrier between them and oppression could not endure half their woes. And how characteristic of human frailties! Here are slave-dealers who weep over the legendary sufferings of a saint, and laugh at worse tortures they themselves inflict; who shudder at the names of old persecutors, and dream not of the armies of martyrs they make yearly; who cry over Protestants as sinners doomed to perdition, and smile in anticipation of their own reception in the realms above by Anthony and Loyala, Benedict and Becket.

As mentioned before, the abolition of slavery did not mean the end of hardships and exploitation of African people in the New World. It also meant an increase in hardships for those still living on the African continent, as Europeans set their sights towards colonizing Africa. This process entailed the subjugation and repression of the native population, much as had been done on the slave plantations in the New World. The native population was also in some cases forced to work under slave like conditions much as Africans in the New World had done.

References:

"An Update on Corporate Slavery," *New York Times* Jan. 31, 2005.

Angelique Chrisafis, "France faces revolt over poverty on its Caribbean islands," *The Guardian*, February 11, 2009.

Anne Bailey, *African Voices of the Atlantic Slave Trade*, (Beacon Press, 2006).

Courtney R. Baker, "Misrecognized: Looking at Images of Black Suffering and Death," 2008. (dissertation)

Eric Williams, *Capitalism and Slavery*, 1944.

___*History of the People of Trinidad and Tobago*, 1962.

Frederick Douglass, *The Narrative of the Life of Frederick Douglass*, 1845.

Hollis Liverpool, "Researching Steelband and Calypso Music in the British Caribbean and the U. S. Virgin Islands," *Black Music Research Journal*, Vol. 14, No. 2 (Autumn, 1994), pp. 179-201

John Coleman De Graft-Johnson, *African Glory: The Story of Vanished Negro Civilizations*, (Black Classic Press, 1986).

John Newton, *The Posthumous Works of the Rev. John Newton*, 1809.

Kristen Stromberg Childers, "Citizenship and Assimilation in Postwar Martinique: The Abolition of Slavery and the Politics of Commemoration," *Citizenship and Assimilation*, Volume 34 (2006).

Lansiné Kaba, "The Atlantic Slave Trade Was Not a 'Black-on-Black Holocaust'", *African Studies Review*, Vol. 44, No. 1 (Apr., 2001), pp. 1-20

Larry Eugene Rivers, *Rebels and Runaways: Slave Resistance in Nineteenth-Century Florida*, (University of Illinois Press, 2012).

Nick Nesbitt, "Departmentalization and the Logic of Decolonization," *L'Esprit Créateur*, Vol. 47, No. 1 (2007), pp. 32–43

Olaudah Equiano, *The Interesting Narrative of the Life of Olaudah Equiano*, 1789.

"Rail networks own lines built with slave labor," *USA Today*, Feb. 21, 2002.

Rex A. Hudson, ed. *Brazil: A Country Study*. 1997

Robert Campbell, *A Pilgrimage in My Motherland: An Account of a Journey Among the Egbas and Yorubas of Central Africa In 1859-1860*, 1861.

Stephanie Smallwood, *Saltwater Slavery: A Middle Passage from Africa to American Diaspora*, (Harvard University Press, 2008).

"The Untold History of Post-Civil War 'Neoslavery,'" Talk of the Nation, March 25, 2008.

Thomas Ewbank, *Life in Brazil*, (Harper & Brothers, Publishers, 1856).

W.E.B. Du Bois, *The Negro*, 1915.

___*The Suppression of the African Slave Trade*, 1896.

Walter Rodney, *A History of the Upper Guinea Coast, 1545 to 1800*, (Oxford University Press, 1970).

___*How Europe Underdeveloped Africa*, (Bogle-L'Ouverture Publications, 1972).

___ *A History of the Guyanese Working People, 1881-1905*, (Johns Hopkins University Press, 1981).

3 PROFITS FROM COLONIZATION

In 1884, the colonial powers sat down at what was known as the Berlin Conference and divided Africa up amongst themselves. The scramble for Africa had begun prior to this conference, but it was at this conference that the European colonialists formally divided Africa between each other. The idea of calling a conference to settle territorial disputes was first suggested by Portugal and then carried out by Otto von Bismarck. No African leaders were present at the conference. Much as the slave trade was carried out by the Europeans with little consideration for the desires of African rulers, so too was colonization a process that was imposed on Africans by Europeans without African consent or input.

The two African nations that were officially not colonized were Liberia and Ethiopia, though Liberia still found its resources being exploited by American capitalists. Ethiopia had managed to escape the initial Italian invasion, but Italy launched a second invasion in 1935 which resulted in Italy briefly ruling Ethiopia. This war is especially known for the Italian usage of poisonous gas. Although they were independent, Liberia and Ethiopia found their interests constantly being undermined by Western nations.

The Europeans divided Africa up by drawing borders that had not previously existed on the continent. They then proceeded to exploit African resources, and used African labor to cultivate those resources. Various corporations benefited from this colonization, including the Lever Brothers soap company which was owned by William H. Lever. Later, the Lever Brothers merged with a Dutch company named Margarine Unie to form Unilever. Unilever profited greatly from using Africa's land and resources.

Cecil Rhodes was a specific individual who became extremely wealthy from his exploits in southern Africa. He founded a diamond company called De Beers. During his business ventures Rhodes stole so much wealth from Africa that he was able to establish the Rhodes Scholarship for students at the Oxford University. Walter Rodney states in *How Europe Underdeveloped Africa* that "Cecil Rhodes could afford to leave a legacy of lavish scholarships to white students for study at Oxford University, having made a fortune from exploiting Africa and Africans." It was through exploitation and violence that Rhodes made his profits. The land that he conquered was even named after him; Northern Rhodesia and Southern Rhodesia. Rhodes' conquest of these regions was a bloody one that resulted in the deaths of many Africans.

In his dealing with the Ndebele ruler Lobengula, Rhodes employed trickery to achieve his goals. Lobengula had been very cautious in his relationship with Europeans, as he recognized that they could be a potential threat to the interests of the Ndebele people. For this reason he restricted European immigration to his nation and informed Europeans that he would not open up his nation to them for mining or hunting. Lobengula moved from town to town to pit Europeans against each other to help protect his nation.

In 1888, Rhodes decided that the best way to bring the Ndebele under European control was to employ the help of Reverend John Smith Moffat. Moffat previously made a failed attempt to convert Lobengula to Christianity and for this reason he was eager to see the colonization of the Ndebele people. Moffat presented himself to Lobengula as a spiritual advisor seeking to give advice to an "old friend." This advice was to ally with the British rather than the Afrikaners, Portuguese or Germans. The agreement that Lobengula signed stipulated that he could not enter into a treaty or correspondence with any foreign nation relating to Ndebeleland without first consulting with the High Commissioner for South Africa. This treaty began the British colonization of Rhodesia and Lobengula had unknowingly brought his nation under British control.

Lobengula could no longer use his tactic of pitting European powers against each other, as he was restricted to dealing solely with the British. British businessmen quickly flocked to Ndebeleland to benefit from the nation's mineral wealth. Rhodes himself was working on securing complete control of Ndebeleland. Moffat was again sent to advise Lobengula. He introduced Lobengula to Rudd, Thompson, and Maguire—three men who were sent on behalf of Rhodes. After four weeks of negotiations, Lobengula signed what became known as the "Rudd Concession." This agreement gave concessionaires complete and exclusive control over the resources of Ndebeleland. Lobengula verbally stated certain conditions of his own, which included limiting the number of white men in his territories to ten at a time, that white men would obey the laws of his country, and that whites would fight in defense of the country under Ndebele command if need be. These verbal conditions were not written into the final agreement, however, and therefore were not enforced. When news of this deal became known, there was fear and confusion amongst the Ndebele people. The Ndebele warriors were furious, and Lobengula was fearful of losing power.

Lobengula immediately took steps to overturn the concession. In the *Bechuanaland News* he published a notice of repudiation in February of 1889. Lobengula also ordered the pro-British *induna* (advisor), Lotshe, be executed along with his family and livestock. Lobengula sent letters directly to the British government, pleading for Queen Victoria to cancel the concession or to declare Ndebeleland as a protectorate. In January of 1889 he had sent an official delegation to London to meet with Queen Victoria. When this failed, Lobengula sent a formal protest in April. He stated that he would not recognize the agreement that he signed, stating: "It was proved to me that I had signed away the mineral rights of my whole country to Rudd and his friends." Despite these attempts, the treaty remained in place. In 1893, the Ndebele finally went to war with the British. Led by Rhodes, the British killed thousands of Ndebele. Lobengula went into exile, where he eventually died.

African resources also contributed to European technological advances. Manganese was mined throughout Africa and was used in the creation of steel. Chrome was mined in South Africa and Southern Rhodesia for the purpose of manufacturing stainless steel. Columbite, which was mined in Nigeria, was used for the creation of steel for jet-engines. The number one mineral export from Africa was copper, which was a critical aspect of the electrical industry in Western nations.

Guinea was used to export bauxite, which would be turned into aluminum. In 1952, Guinea earned France 1 billion francs, but the benefit France received from the colonies was not merely financial. African soldiers were employed in various wars for the French, including World War II and France's war against the Vietnamese. Needless to say, most of the profits France was earning from Guinea were not shared with the Africans. The British colonial administration mined gold in Chunya, Tanganyika. This process began in 1933. By 1953, the gold supply was finished and Chunya was one of the poorest locations in Tanganyika.

European exploitation of African resources also led to the creation of "monoculture" economies or nations which were dependent on the production of a single crop or resource. African nations often produced whatever was beneficial to the colonialists and this mode of economic production severely limited the potential of post-colonial African nations. For instance, the colonial Gold Coast produced cocoa. In the independent Ghana (formerly the Gold Coast), cocoa remained the main export, although Kwame Nkrumah worked towards diversifying Ghana's agriculture. Groundnuts accounted for as much as 90% of the revenue of Senegal and Gambia. Liberia was dependent on rubber.

In general, Africans were paid for their labor,—apart from the cases of forced slave labor, which will be discussed later—but this pay was so insignificant that the Africans were working for almost nothing. For example, in Uganda the African peasants worked for hours to cultivate cotton and they were paid so little that the price of the finished cotton shirt was more than they could even afford. One French official remarked: "I have always noticed that whenever the budget of a native family was properly and regularly kept, it never managed to make ends meet. The life of a native is, in fact, a miracle." The lack of pay that Nigerian workers received resulted in strikes such as the 1949 Enugu coal mine strike. In one of the areas where the miners were striking the police opened fire, killing 21 miners and injuring 51.

Africans were also given little compensation for whatever

losses that they endured. In 1934 when 41 Africans were killed in a gold mine accident in the Gold Coast, their families were given 3 pounds each as compensation. On top of the poor pay and lack of compensation, Africans were also heavily taxed. These taxes, along with the little pay that the Africans received, allowed the Europeans to recover for the military costs of conquering Africa and maintaining their colonies. In essence, Africans were paying for their own exploitation. The Europeans would tax certain items such as cattle, houses, and in some cases the people were taxed.

There were also instances in which Africans were forced to work against their will. Africans were forced, by various methods, to work for the Europeans. One means of forcing Africans to work for the colonies was by controlling the food supply. In colonies such as Kenya and Rhodesia, the Africans were banned from growing cash-crops so that their labor was used solely for the Europeans. In French Equatorial Africa the French banned the Mandja people from hunting and they were forced to turn their attention to cultivating cotton. Colonel Grogan, a settler in Kenya, stated of the Kikuyu: "We have stolen his land. Now we must steal his limbs. Compulsory labour is the corollary of our occupation of the country." The Maasai people in Kenya also lost their land to the white settlers and they were forced to relocate to settlements. The colonial government claimed that the Maasai had agreed to surrender their land, but when the Maasai challenged this in court the court ruled against them.

In Uganda the Acholi revolted in 1911. This revolt was in response to attempts to both recruit the Acholi for labor purposes, as well as to disarm them. The British colonial government wanted to collect all of the firearms that the Acholi possessed, but the Acholi were unwilling. The revolt was put down, but it demonstrated how the colonial government attempted to strip the ability of African people to resist exploitation.

Forced labor was used in Nigeria, although it was often met with resistance on the part of the Africans. Harold Moray Douglas forced the Igbo to build roads and houses for colonial officers. Those who refused were punished and Douglas paid little attention to the poor treatment of the workers. In one instance a chief named Nwogu was ordered to supply forced labor for the colony. When he complied, some of his people allegedly rose up in rebellion and killed him. When no suspects were produced, Douglas decided to attack the Norie to prove to the people that his orders were not to be disobeyed. The Norie were prepared to defend themselves and in the resulting war many of the Norie were killed. Houses and farms were also destroyed.

In another instance, the Eziama refused to make roads as Douglas had instructed. Douglas responded by attacking the Eziama and destroying all of their houses. The chiefs were ordered to force their people to construct the roads, but many refused. Douglas responded by capturing the Eziama chiefs in an attempt to make the people comply. This forced the Eziama to build the roads.

Forced labor was enforced in the Portuguese colonies. The Portuguese dictator Antonio Salazar stated that Portugal's "New State" would be built by the labor of "inferior peoples." As such, some of the worst instances of forced labor and colonial abuses occurred in the Portuguese controlled colonies. In Mozambique, men were required to pay 100 pounds of cotton and women were required to pay 50 pounds. Those who failed were punished with a stick known as the *palmatoria*. Captain Henrique Galvão served in an official capacity for more than two decades in Angola. He documented the various abuses that were inflicted against the Africans. The Salazar government arrested Galvão for doing so. They charged him with treason and they banned his report. There were some labor reforms in the late 1940s, but throughout the 1950s forced labor continued. It was only in 1962 that forced labor was abolished.

Another aspect of Salazar's policies in Angola was to suppress any form of political dissent. African informants were frequently employed to handle this task. The growth of African leadership in Angola was stunted by censorship and colonial control of education. Africans from Angola and Mozambique were also exported to South Africa to work in the mines. The Portuguese government received payment for the laborer that they supplied to South Africa and this practice was so extensive that in 1903 Mozambique provided about 89 percent of the labor force for South African mines.

Kwame Nkrumah gave the following description of labor in Africa under colonialism:

Under colonialism, African workers have no effective bargaining power. Trade unions are frequently disallowed by law, and they are largely unorganized. They have either to accept the pitifully low wages offered to them or suffer the consequences of being without work, which, in certain regimes, makes them liable to a variety of punishments. In South Africa, under the gruesome regulations of *apartheid*, the African worker is hounded and forced into conditions of helotry. Shameful as these are, conditions for Africans in the Portuguese territories probably surpass them though they have not so far received such attention from critics.

The forced labor that Africans endured was brutal. In some cases the magnitude of the work was so much that it was fatal to many of the Africans workers—mirroring the working conditions that Africans endured on the slave plantations in the Americas. In Sierra Leone, thousands of African peasants were made to build a railway. The working conditions were so harsh that many of them died. In 1921 the French used African labor to begin building the Brazzaville to Pointe-Noire railway. Every year they would drive 10,000 people to work at this site. This project was not finished until 1933, and during that time at least 25% of the labor force died annually from starvation and disease.

In Ivory Coast, the French imposed a system of forced labor that required each adult male to work ten days a year without compensation. This was seen as each man's obligation to the state. The French also recruited workers from the Upper Volta to work in Ivory Coast as well due to a shortage of Ivorian workers. This practice of forced labor was made worse during World War II after the fall of France. The Vichy government subjected French West Africa to intense economic exploitation. Labor recruitment and military conscription intensified. African farmers were also forced to meet quotas to supply the armed forces. Ivorians grew to resent the Vichy regime.

One of the worst cases of forced African labor occurred in German South-West Africa. The Germans saw this colony as a suitable location for settlement to deal with the overcrowding of Berlin's slums. The Germans also viewed themselves as being superior to the African natives. The Africans were abused and often used as slave labor by the German colonialists. African women were also raped by the Germans.

The Herero people began rebelling against German injustices. They killed hundreds of German settlers within a matter of days. In response to these rebellions, German troops opened fire on an unarmed Herero mission station in Otjimbingwe, despite the fact that the Herero there were not even involved in the previous uprisings. Soon these revolts gave way to a war between the Germans and the Herero. The Herero did not want to pursue a long term war with the Germans, however. The Herero people moved away from the German settlements and hoped for a peace negotiation with the Germans. Instead of a negotiation, the Germans were preparing an army with the intention of wiping out the Herero people.

German propaganda was set up to gain public support for this massacre of the Herero people. The Germans made it appear as though the Herero were a savage and violent people that needed to be confronted with military force. German cartoons also depicted the Herero as being particularly violent towards white women, when this was not actually the case. At the Battle of Waterberg the Germans decisively defeated the Herero. The German general Lothar von Trotha then gave the infamous annihilation order. He planned the extermination of all the Herero people, claiming that he would no longer accept women or children.

Many of the Herero were driven into the desert where they died from starvation and thirst. It was also during this massacre that the Germans opened their first concentration camps. The Germans rounded up the surviving Herero and forced them into these camps. The Herero people were given a number and identified by this number. In these camps the Herero were used as slave labor. Many died of overwork and exhaustion. Others were shot or beaten. In these camps, food was scarce and the prisoners were given no medical care. The Nama people revolted against German rule and suffered the same fate as the Herero people had.

The German army began renting Herero prisoners to private companies. Some private companies were so large that they ran their own camps. One of these camps was run by the Woermann shipping company, which had their own supply of Herero slaves working for them. Slavery was legally abolished for Africans in the New World, but African people in Africa were still very much being enslaved under colonization. The Germans also enforced a policy of forced labor in other colonies, such as German East Africa. The Maji Maji rebellion was yet another rebellion in response to the horrible treatment that the Africans suffered under German rule.

The exploitation of the Congo was unique in that the Congo (or Congo Free State as it was known) became the personal property of King Leopold II of Belgium. Leopold was eager to acquire a colony, and with the help of an explorer known as Henry Stanley, Leopold was able to claim the Congo. Leopold had the reputation of being a "philanthropic" monarch, but his rule over the Congo suggests otherwise. Leopold also established the International African Association for his humanitarian projects in Central Africa. Leopold's mission in the Congo was portrayed as a civilizing mission with the goal of countering the Arab slave trade in the region.

An African American named George Washington Williams wrote an open letter to Leopold II over the poor treatment of the Africans in the Congo. Williams was a Civil War veteran who was frustrated with the brutal treatment of blacks in the United States. He was especially frustrated that he fought in a war which ended slavery, but did not end racism in America. Williams also became quite an accomplished historian. W.E.B. Du Bois referred to him as "the greatest historian of the race."

When Williams met with Leopold, he was impressed by him. While discussing the Congo, Leopold had said to him, "What I do there is done as a Christian duty to the poor African; and I do not wish to have one franc back of all the money I have expended." Williams bought into this idea that Leopold was a great and noble Christian monarch who wished "to promote the best interests of his subjects, ruling in wisdom, mercy, and justice." Williams was eagerly seeking to gather a number of African Americans to work in Africa, but when he expressed his ideas at a black college in Virginia, he found that they were skeptical. They also had questions about life in Africa that Williams could not answer. Williams decided to postpone his recruiting plans and go to the Congo to gather material to write a book.

In his open letter to Leopold, Williams presented a carefully researched account of some of the atrocities that were taking place. This letter caused a strong reaction from Leopold and the Belgian press. Among the attacks hurled at Williams was the fact that Williams claimed to be a colonel when he was in fact not one. The Belgian press also called him "an unbalanced negro." Despite the hostile reaction to Williams' allegations, some Belgian newspapers did point out that Leopold was an autocrat ruling over a country that he had never stepped foot in. They felt that this was bound to cause a certain number of abuses.

One historian noted that Williams' death on August 2, 1891 "saved the Congo government from what might have been an embarrassingly formidable opponent." Not only was Williams not a colonel, but he had claimed to have a doctorate that he did not really have, and it was only after his death that his British fiancée learned that he abandoned his wife and son in the United States. Williams was not known to be a very honest man, but his work set the stage for others who sought to expose the abuses in the Congo.

Much like he told Williams, Leopold continued to maintain that the purpose of his rule of the Congo was not monetary profits, when this was in fact what was happening. He spoke about using methods to shake the "cannibals" from "their idleness and make them realize the sanctity of work." Among the riches that Leopold hoped to find in the Congo was ivory. Africans in the Congo were banned from selling ivory to anyone other than Leopold's agents.

Leopold established the Force Publique, an army of paid mercenaries that was to defend his interests in the Congo. Powerful military force was necessary for the people of the Congo were not easily subdued. The military conquests of the Force Publique were justified as being expeditions that were meant to pacify the natives. The Belgian colonizers were also able to take advantage of pre-existing rivalries to pit one group of Africans against another before ultimately conquering both parties. The usage of such divide and conquer tactics was common throughout the period of European colonial rule in Africa.

The Force Publique had to deal with various rebellions from the colonized people. It took ten years to subdue the Yaka people, while the Chokwe fought for twenty years. The Boa and Budja people mobilized five thousand men to fight Leopold's forces. The Sanga people were led by Chief Mulume Niama, who refused to

Dwayne Wong (Omowale)

surrender to the Force Publique. Another chief named Nzansu launched an attack that destroyed various posts that had been set up by the Belgians, but he spared the missionaries. One of the missionaries wrote back home saying: "The leader of the rebels, Chief Nzansu of Kasi, has let us know that he does not wish harm to any one of us as we have always shown that we are friends of the black people. But to the men of the State he has sworn death."

Resistance in the Congo continued even after Leopold lost control of his territory. Simon Kimbangu, who was a carpenter who converted to Christianity, led a religious movement in the Belgian Congo. Inspired by a dream he had in 1921, Kimbangu called for Africans to leave the European missionaries and establish independent churches. Africans eagerly abandoned the European churches and flocked to Kimbangu.

The Belgians were becoming increasingly concerned with the growing popularity of Kimbangu. Many of his followers would leave the plantations for religious meetings, which meant that many key functions for the colonial government were not getting done. Some of Kimbangu's followers decided that they would no longer pay taxes. This religious movement also drew a following among those who were from the British and French colonies. In 1921 the government called for Kimbangu's arrest.

Kimbangu managed to escape at first, which made him more popular among the masses. He stayed in one village where he was visited by thousands of followers. He was eventually captured and tried by the colonial government. He was accused of trying to overthrow the Belgian government and of using religion to incite the masses. Kimbangu was sentenced to death. Among Kimbangu's followers who were imprisoned included a woman named Mandobe. She received a two year sentence.

The news of Kimbangu's death sentence caused strikes throughout the Congo. This became so disruptive that some proposed to have Kimbangu publicly hanged. The Africans in turn claimed that if Kimbangu was killed it would be followed by a massacre of white people. Kimbangu's sentence was commuted to a sentence of life imprisonment. Kimbangu remained in prison until his death in 1951, but Kimbangu continued to have a religious following in the Congo.

Kimbangu's movement was significant in that it laid the basis for the anti-colonial movement in the Congo. Kimbangu's followers saw him as a messiah who would deliver them from European oppression. Out of this movement came the slogan, "Congo to the Congolese." His followers were firm in their belief that Kimbangu would "return to bring white domination to an end."

Under the Force Publique many abuses occurred. They enslaved the Africans and used them for labor. Each worker was given a quota to meet and those who failed to meet their quota had their hands amputated. African Force Publique soldiers were rewarded for the amount of hands that they collected. Whippings, rape, and mass murder was also common under Force Publique rule. In order to force the African men to work, their wives were taken as hostages.

Among those who were forced to work were children. Children as young as seven were made to carry loads of twenty-two pounds. For punishment, children were lined up and flogged. In one instance a number of boys had laughed in the presence of a white man, which prompted him to order that all the servant boys in the town to be given fifty lashes. One of the most dreaded forms of punishment were blows delivered from a chicotte. Very often Africans were used to inflict chicotte beatings on other Africans.

The situation in the Congo became so dire that hundreds of thousands of people fled their villages to escape the Belgian soldiers. The soldiers often responded to this by burning the huts and crops, and taking animals to leave Africans without any food. Africans were so desperate not to get captured that sometimes children were abandoned out of fear that their cries would give away their hiding places. Many children starved to death for this reason. Those who lived near the Congo's borders escaped into other countries. In 1900, the French colonial governor estimated that 30,000 refugees from the Congo were living in French territory.

In the 1890s there was a boom in rubber. Leopold had gone in debt with the investments he made in the Congo, but with the demand for rubber Leopold was now making a fortune from his colony, while engaging in a propaganda war to cover up what was truly going on in the Congo Free State. Reports from African Americans who went to the Congo, such as George Washington

Williams and William Henry Sheppard, were dismissed by Leopold. Leopold would not be able to keep the atrocities a secret for long however. Europe began to pay close attention to what was going on in the Congo when an Irish man named Stokes was murdered by a Congo officer. The leading figure in exposing the crimes that were happening in the Congo was a British journalist named E.D. Morel. Leopold was eventually forced to turn over his colony to the Belgian government. Even by the terrible standards of colonial rule, Leopold's abuses were shocking to the Europeans.

Though the Belgian government now had control of the Congo, the atrocities would not truly end. The Africans were still beaten, mistreated, and discriminated against in their own homeland. For this reason it should be no surprise that Patrice Lumumba was not so willing to forget the brutalities inflicted by the Belgians when the Congo was finally granted its independence from Belgian colonial rule.

The Belgian Congo also played a significant role for Belgium and the other Allies during World War II. It was from the Congo that most of the uranium used in making the atomic bombs for World War II was acquired. The Congo was also useful in regard to helping Belgium recover after World War II. After Belgium was overtaken by the Germans, a Belgian government was established in London. The Colonial Secretary of that government said:

> During the war, the Congo was able to finance all the expenditure of the Belgian government in London, including the diplomatic service as well as the cost of our armed forces in Europe and Africa, a total of some 40 million pounds. In fact, thanks to the resources of the Congo, the Belgian government in London had not to borrow a shilling or a dollar, and the Belgian gold reserve could be left intact.

Most of the infrastructure that was built in Africa was built solely for the enjoyment of the Europeans. This was especially the case with colonies like Kenya and South Africa, where a significant amount of Europeans were living as settlers. The Europeans living in their African colonies wanted to live in luxury at the expense of the Africans. The Indians who came to work in the British colonies also lived in better conditions than the Africans. In other words, the Africans were at the bottom of the social structure in their own countries.

The colonial powers, although largely indifferent to the suffering of those in the colonies, were nevertheless aware that suffering was taking place. After having investigated rioting in the West Indies, the British established the Colonial Development and Welfare Act (CD&W) to better provide for these colonies. The French also established a similar program known as *Fonds d'Investissements pour le Developement Économique et Social* (FIDES). The CD & W and FIDES did not really achieve much in the way of improving the poverty of those who were oppressed under British and French colonization, but it was good for propaganda purposes. It created the illusion that the Europeans really cared for the well-being of their colonial subjects. Walter Rodney explains: "As colonialism came under heavy criticism during the last decades, more deliberate efforts were made to whitewash it. Both CD&W and FIDES were part of the public relations propaganda of colonialism, striving to mask and deny its viciousness."

By the end of the colonial period in Africa, a number of businesses and industries had enriched themselves through the usage of African resources. Africans, on the other hand, were exploited. They were forced to work, often against their will, for the benefit of the European colonialists. African workers either made very little money or made to work by force for no pay at all. By the time that African nations had become independent, they were, for the most part, still reliant on the former colonial powers. The political situation had changed, but the economic one remained the same.

Dwayne Wong (Omowale)

References:

A. Abu Boahen (editor), *General History of Africa VII: African Under Colonial Domination 1880-1935*, (University of California Press, 1985).

Adam Hochschild, *King Leopold's Ghost*, (New York: Mariner Books, 1998).

Barbara Harrell-Bond and Sarah Forer, "Guinea-Bissau Part 1: The Colonial Experience," *American Universities Field Staff Reports*, 1981.

Kwame Nkrumah, *Africa Must Unite*, (Frederick A. Praeger, 1963).

Robert E. Handloff (editor), *Côte d'Ivoire: A Country Study*, Washington: GPO for the Library of Congress, 1991.

Namibia: Genocide and the Second Reich, 2005.

Marvin Pery, Joseph R. Penden, Theodore H. Von Laue, George W. Bock (editors), *Sources of the Western Tradition: Volume II: From the Renaissance to the Present*, (Wadsworth, Cengage Learning, 2008).

Thomas Collelo (editor), *Angola: A Country Study*, Washington: GPO for the Library of Congress, 1991.

Toyin Falola, *Colonialism and Violence in Nigeria*, (Indiana University Press, 2009).

Walter Rodney, *How Europe Underdeveloped Africa*, (Bogle-L'Ouverture Publications, 1972).

4 THE IMPACT OF COLONIALISM AND BEYOND

One of the justifications for colonizing Africa was the idea that the Europeans were modernizing or civilizing Africa. One British statesman named Joseph Chamberlain argued: "We feel now that our rule over these territories can only be justified if we can show that it adds to the happiness and prosperity of the people and I maintain that our rule does, and has, brought security and peace and comparative prosperity to countries that never knew these blessings before." This assertion is a curious one given that British rule of a particular colony was typically achieved through warfare and conquest. Chamberlain himself recognized this, stating that "in the first instance, when these conquests have been made, there has been bloodshed, there has been loss of life among the native populations, loss of still more precious lives among those who have been sent out to bring these countries into some kind of disciplined order [...]." The reference to the lives of the colonialists that were being sent out to conquer Africa as being "more precious" is revealing. Even more revealing is that Chamberlain would justify this violence by arguing that "you cannot destroy the practices of barbarism, of slavery, of superstition, which for centuries have desolated the interior of Africa, without the use of force" and "that for one life lost a hundred will be gained, and the cause of civilisation and the prosperity of the people will in the long run be eminently advanced."

Admittedly, colonization did have somewhat of a modernizing

impact, although the overall "benefits" of colonialism are offset by the many negative features of colonialism. As was established in the previous chapters, Europe's economic rise was truly sparked though the exploitation of Africans and other people. Therefore, the Europeans had already been in the process of undermining and destroying African people prior to the colonization of Africa. Once the Europeans did colonize Africa, the "benefits" of modernization only benefitted a handful of Africans. The vast majority lived in a state of stagnation and poverty. Walter Rodney explained that the "sum total of these services was amazingly small."

In the process of conquering Africa many African leaders were often deposed and robbed of whatever wealth they acquired. Two cases of this were Jaja of Opobo and Nana Olomu, both of whom lived in what would become the British colony of Nigeria. They both were wealthy traders who were exiled by the British because the colonialists saw these men as being a threat to Britain's own trade interests in the region. Jubo Jubogha, best known as Jaja of Opobo, was born in about 1821 in the Orlu district of Eastern Nigeria. He was known as one of the most enterprising and accomplished African merchants in West Africa. Jaja was originally an Igbo slave who was sold in Bonny. He earned his freedom and became a very skilled merchant, so much so that his skill even impressed his enemies. Jaja eventually broke away from Bonny and established a successful trading center at Opobo in 1869.

Jaja was forced to leave Bonny when his success invoked the jealousy of the Manilla Pepple House. This house included Oko Jumbo, who was a wealthy and influential chief in Bonny. Oko Jumbo considered waging a civil war to overthrow Jaja. Jaja, recognizing that he was both outnumbered and outgunned, refused to be dragged into a civil war. When his attempts at negotiating a peaceful resolution to the conflict failed, Jaja was forced to retreat and establish a kingdom of his own.

Jaja had a great understanding of Western culture. He was fluent in English and had sent one of his sons to a Glasgow school. Jaja also established his own school in Opobo. One of the teachers of this school was Emma White. She was born in Kentucky to slave parents. White later changed her name to Emma Jaja.

Alexander Cowan said of Jaja:

He could be stern, and he was strict, but he was always just, and the form of government he set up was as near perfect as anything of its kind could be. Every man had the right of appeal, and, though in effect his own authority was never questioned, he conformed to his own rules, and governed through his council of chiefs.

Jaja also demonstrated outstanding leadership qualities. Mary Kingsley, a woman who explored West Africa in 1893 and 1894, explained that Jaja was elected by the elders of House of Annie Pepple to be the chief following the death of Elolly Pepple. Elolly left behind a lot of debt, which Jaja managed to pay off in two years. Kingsley described:

Ja Ja had not been many months head of the Annie Pepple House before he began to show the old chiefs what kind of metal he was made of; for during the first twelve months he had selected from amongst the late Elolly's slaves no less than eighteen or twenty young men, who had already amassed a little wealth, and whom he thought capable of being trusted to trade on their own account, bought canoes for them, took them to the European traders, got them to advance each of these young men from five to ten puncheons worth of goods, he himself standing guarantee for them. This operation had the effect of making Ja Ja immediately popular amongst all classes of the slaves of the late chief. At the same time, the slaves of the old chief of the House began to see that there was a man at the head of the House who would set a good example to their immediate masters. Some of these young men are now wealthy chiefs in Opobo, and as evidence that they had been well chosen, Ja Ja was never called upon to fulfil his guarantee.

Jaja's policies frustrated British firms. He aligned himself only with Alexander Miller Brother and Company because Alexander Miller agreed to trade on Jaja's terms. Prior to this Jaja had ceased trade with the British traders in his kingdom completely. Jaja's partnership with Alexander Miller led to fierce competition between the British trading firms in the region. By 1884 other British firms felt that Jaja was profiting at their expense, so they came together and fixed the price of produce. Jaja responded to this by becoming the first Nigerian direct exporter of palm oil, shipping his product to Birmingham. From this wealth Jaja built up a military force, which he later sent to help the British in the Asante War in 1875. For his support Jaja received a sword of honor from Queen Victoria.

British traders began looking for ways to counter Jaja's role as a middle-man. For this they sought the help of the British Consul. In 1884, Consul Hewett asked Jaja to sign a treaty which placed his territory under British control. Jaja agreed, but only under the condition that the clause which gave the European traders free trade and free access to the territory would be removed. Hewett reluctantly agreed, but a year later the British declared a Protectorate over the Gulf of Guinea. Jaja responded to this action by completely rejecting the provisions for free trade.

The British accused Jaja of organizing armed attacks that obstructed trade. The new Vice-Consul Harry Johnston called for Jaja's deportation in 1887. The British Foreign Office approved. Johnston invited Jaja for a discussion and promised that Jaja would get to leave, but this was not so. Jaja was taken to Accra where he was tried and then sentenced to deportation for five years in the West Indies. Jaja, with the help of Major Macdonald, got the sentence revoked, but he died on his way back home.

The British faced similar problems with another wealthy merchant named Nana Olomu. Nana Olomu was an Itsekiri who was born around 1852. Nana's father was a rich and powerful merchant, but Nana did not rely solely on this inherited wealth. He was a great state builder and in many ways could be compared to Jaja. One British official even referred to Nana as the Jaja of the West Delta, noting that Nana was probably even wealthier than Jaja was. Like Jaja, Nana dictated his own trade terms.

Between 1886 and 1887, Nana held up palm oil exports when the price of palm oil fell by 40%. This was done to force the Europeans to accept the terms that were laid down by the local producers and suppliers. In 1891 the British opened up a Vice-Consulate at Sapele that was separate from the one that they had on the Benin River. This was done to undermine Nana and to reduce the trade on the Benin River, which was the main source of Nana's wealth. He responded by sending agents to Sapele. The British found that Nana's agents were in firm control of the trade. Like Jaja, Nana did not agree to a clause that would allow the British traders to have free access to trade in his kingdom. Nana's influence over the trade of the region was a threat to British interests in the region and because he proved to be uncooperative, the British sought to reduce his power.

Major Claude Macdonald, the British Commissioner and Consul General for Oil Rivers Protectorate, reported that when he met with Nana, Nana arrived in a war canoe that was paddled by about 100 people. Four or five similar canoes escorted Nana's canoe and he had twenty armed men with Winchester repeater rifles. This led Macdonald to proclaim that Nana was "a man possessed of great power and wealth, astute, energetic and intelligent." It was said that Nana had a fleet of 200 trade canoes and 100 war canoes. Among Nana's supplies that were seized after he was defeated were 106 cannons, 445 blunderbusses, 640 guns, 10 revolvers, 1640 kegs of gunpowder, and 2500 rounds of machine gun ammunition.

The British falsely accused him of disrupting commercial activities in the Niger Delta and of terrorizing the Urhobo and turning them against the British. They also accused him of trafficking slaves and practicing human sacrifice—all of which were lies. The reality was that the British were looking for a justification to take action against Nana. In 1894, the British laid siege to Ebrohimi, which caused Nana to fortify his capital. Though Nana was eventually defeated, he put up a brilliant resistance. The British expected an easy expedition, but they ended up facing one of their most difficult and costly expeditions in West Africa, for Nana masterfully combined conventional warfare with guerilla tactics, as well as utilizing his knowledge of the creeks that the British had to sail to reach Ebrohimi. Nana refused to surrender and his memory of what happened to Jaja did not permit Nana to meet with the British for a discussion.

All the attempts by the British to take Ebrohimi by going up the creek failed. On three occasions they were forced to withdraw after suffering heavy casualties. The British finally discovered the best route to Ebrohimi and on September 25, 1894, Nana was defeated. He was tried and exiled to Ghana. His goods were also sold and the proceeds were used to pay for the cost of the expedition. Both Jaja and Nana were wealthy kings who lost their trading empires due to the greed and economic interests of the European colonizers. The European conquest of Africa was not a peaceful one. It was a rather bloody one which often stripped African people of their wealth.

One of the advantages that the European colonizers had was the lack of unity on the part of Africans. African rulers were well-aware that neighboring kingdoms were being conquered, but very rarely did African rulers unite to face this threat. As pointed out previously, Jaja had helped the British in their war against the Asante people with no consideration for the reality that Opobo could similarly be conquered by the British. Mary Kingsley described the situation this way:

> Thus the fall of Ashantee in 1873 was well known to the King of Dahomey, yet he continued on his way and could not believe the French could ever upset him. Nana, the governor of the lower Benin or Jakri, could not see in the downfall of Ja Ja that the British Government were not to be trifled with by any petty king or governor of these rivers; though Nana was a most intelligent native, he had the temerity to show fight against the Protectorate officials, and of course he quickly found out his mistake, but alas! too late for his peace of mind and happiness; he is now a prisoner at large far away from his own country, stripped of all his riches and position.

In 1903, the British attacked the Sokoto caliphate. After the Sokoto caliphate suffered a defeat at the hands of the British, Muhammadu Attahiru I fled to the east. The British colonialists were still concerned about Attahiru's actions. It was not clear what Attahiru was planning, though some believed that he was planning to continue fighting the British. The British were also troubled by the fact that Attahiru still had strong support, even among the lower classes such as slaves and poor farmers. The British were shocked that the exiled king enjoyed such strong support, especially since they wanted to portray their invasion as one meant to liberate the poor people of Sokoto. As Attahiru I traveled, along the way people donated horses and food for him to demonstrate their loyalty.

For five months the British chased Attahiru before catching up to him at Burmi. The British lost the first battle at Burmi, but Attahiru pleaded that he be allowed to continue his pilgrimage to the east. The British ignored this request and sent an even better organized colonial army to Burmi to attack Attahiru. After an hours long battle, the British were triumphant and Attahiru was among those who were killed. Attahiru's son, Mai Wurno, continued moving eastward and eventually settled in the Sudan.

The Hehe Wars bear mentioning in detail for it was among one of the most successful anti-colonial wars that was fought by Africans against their European colonizers. The two sides came into conflict at a time that they were both seeking to expand their empires. The Hehe under the leadership of Mkwawa were expanding towards the coast. Mkwawa successfully conquered a number of neighboring people to expand his empire. There were others, such as the Ndamba, which submitted to the Hehe without a fight. In return, Mkwawa allowed the Ndamba to keep their rulers, as long as those rulers respected Mkwawa's supremacy.

Mkwawa was known as *Mahinya* (the slaughterer) for his violent behavior. The Germans considered Mkwawa a despot and believed that in deposing him they were freeing his subjects from his rule. In fact, a number of subjects were relieved to be free of Mkwawa's rule. Mkwawa's ruthlessness did serve its purpose in war, however. Many Hehe were afraid to surrender to the Germans because they did not believe that the Germans could protect them from Mkwawa's wrath. Furthermore, many remained loyal to Mkwawa even after the fall of Kalenga, so Mkwawa was not as unpopular as the Germans made him appear.

At the time that the Hehe were expanding towards the coast, the Germans were expanding inland. Eventually the Germans and the Hehe came into a conflict of interests over the expansion of their control in the region. Initially, the Germans attempted to negotiate a peaceful settlement with the Hehe. The Hehe arrived to negotiate with Governor Ramsay. When the negotiations were over the Germans assumed that the Hehe left with peaceful intentions.

This peace was undermined when, in June 1891, the Germans heard reports that the Mafiti people were conducting raids and that a Hehe chief named Taramakengwe was taking prisoners. The Germans dispatched an expedition to deal with the Mafiti first, but they did not find them. Due to lack of food, the Germans troops were forced to alter their plans and they made their way to a place called Usagara. The Hehe rulers in the area fled and the Germans burnt down the abandoned huts. The Germans then made their way to Uhehe, where the Hehe people once again fled. The Germans destroyed more huts and then moved towards Kalenga, where Mkwawa had established a fort.

On their way to Kalenga, the Germans were attacked. This attack, which officially started the conflict between the Germans and the Hehe, was a successful attack. The Hehe also set fire to the dry grass, to burn to death any wounded German soldiers that were unable to flee. Although the attack was a success, a number of Hehe died in the assault. Mkwawa prohibited the mourning of those who were killed to maintain the morale of the survivors.

The governor called on the missionaries to help in negotiations with the Hehe. While the missionaries were assuring the Hehe that the Germans only wanted peace, the Germans were building up garrisons to protect themselves from future attacks. Rather than making peace, the Hehe once again attacked on October 6, 1892. This time they attacked a caravan. The Germans at the time did not send any large expeditions to combat the Hehe. Mkwawa, in the meantime, focused his attention on raiding Africans that had submitted to German rule.

In 1894, the Germans finally sent out a large expedition against the Hehe. They attacked the Kalenga fort on October 30. The ensuing battle was a violent one that lasted many hours. During the chaos a number of Hehe fled, including Mkwawa. By that evening the Germans had taken control of the fort. As the Germans made their return to the coast, the Hehe attempted a failed ambush. During the fall of Kalenga, some Hehe stated that Mkwawa actually went mad and ordered them to put gun-powder without bullets into their guns. Moreover, it appears as if Mkwawa actually wanted to die in the fort.

Apparently Mkwawa tried to blow up the fort with himself inside. Some of the warriors asked him "Do you want to die in the house as if you were a woman?" They forcibly dragged Mkwawa outside of the fort. They fled into the forest and according to oral tradition, after escaping the fort Mkwawa later sat down and cried. When he reached Usungwa he threw away his fly switch. This location was later known as *Itagautwa* ("where he throws away the chiefship"). Some speculate that at this moment Mkwawa wanted to die. Mkwawa had a reputation for being ruthless and at times apparently even mad. In fact, one of his nicknames was *Lukwale-lwa-mwaka* (madness of the year). This perhaps explains his sometimes erratic behavior.

Having destroyed the Kalenga fort, the Germans hoped that Mkwawa would negotiate peace with them, but the Hehe continued their attacks against their neighbors. By 1896, the Germans built a garrison. The expedition was led by Tom von Prince. A few weeks after Prince's arrival, Mkwawa agreed to surrender four of his close relatives, including his younger brother, Mpangile. The Germans hoped this meant that they could come up with a peaceful settlement. The Germans wanted to rule the Hehe through Mpangile, but Tom von Prince blamed Mpangile for continued Hehe attacks on German patrols. Prince had Mpangile tried and executed on February 21, 1897, along with the three other relatives that had surrendered. The Germans then continued their campaign against Mkwawa, who was likely responsible for the attacks that were blamed on Mpangile.

Within a span of 18 months, the Hehe were weakened. Many had surrendered and others had been killed during the fighting. The Germans eventually managed to locate Mkwawa, but by the time they found him he had committed suicide in order to avoid being captured. The death of Mkwawa marked the end of the resistance of the Hehe. In 1897, Mkwawa had told his loyal friends that he would sooner kill himself with his last bullet than surrender to the Germans and this is precisely what he did. Seven years after fighting the Hehe, the Germans had to contend with the Maji Maji revolt, which was mentioned previously. The Hehe people actually sided with the Germans in the rebellion, which demonstrated how the colonialists were able to pit Africans against each other in order to better maintain their control of their colonies.

In Uganda the British clashed with Kabarega, the king of Bunyoro from 1891 until 1899. After being defeated in clashes with the British, Kabarega attempted to use diplomacy to settle his disputes. On two occasions he attempted to make peace with F. D. Lugard. Mwanga, who was the ruler of Buganda, also attempted to intercede on behalf of Kabarega, but this was not successful. With diplomacy having failed, Kabarega turned to guerilla warfare. Kabarega withdrew from Bunyoro and relocated to a country named Lango, where he began a campaign of harassment against the British forces. One British official complained:

> Kabarega was at his old tricks—giving every possible trouble but never standing up for a fair fight, preferring to pursue his favourite methods of assassination. Kabarega caused poison to be given to a friendly chief and he died, but I have had the poisoner killed.

Mwanga eventually joined Kabarega in Lango. The two were finally captured in 1899. Kabarega was captured by Kakunguru, a Muganda general who was working for the British colonists, demonstrating the important role that African agents played in the colonial conquests of Africa. Kakunguru assisted in the spread of British rule in northern and eastern Uganda.

Mwanga's resistance towards colonialism is worth noting in its own right. Mwanga came to the throne as the *Kabaka* of Buganda in 1894. That same year Buganda was declared a British Protectorate. Mwanga was suspicious of the Europeans, especially the Christian missionaries. Mwanga had recognized that the Christian missionaries were an aspect of Europe's attempts of colonial control. For this reason, he attempted to restrict the spread of Christianity in his kingdom. This included killing those who converted to Christianity—the Christians killed by Mwanga came to be viewed as martyrs. Mwanga did not use violence alone to resist the growing foreign influence in his kingdom. He exploited the differences between the Christians and the Muslims by switching his alliance between the two depending on which one he felt was the greatest threat to his rule at any given time.

Mwanga also engaged in guile in his attempt to maintain his rule. In 1888 he plotted to lure the foreigners and their Baganda followers to a naval parade on an island on Lake Victoria, where he intended to leave them stranded to starve to death. This plan was leaked, however. The foreigners responded by deposing Mwanga and putting his brother on the throne, but Mwanga managed to regain power by 1889. After Mwanga was captured, he was exiled where he died in 1903.

The colonialists depicted the kingdoms in Uganda as being ruled by oppressive and despotic African kings. Sinicus described the commoners in Uganda as being "little better than serfs or slaves," which was not an inaccurate depiction. The rulers of Buganda, especially, developed a reputation for cruelty among the Europeans. James Frederick Cunningham recalled seeing a man in Buganda have his ears cut off because his goat nibbled a blade of corn on the king's land. Even the king's own wives were not safe from such brutal discipline. Cunningham also recounted an incident in which Mutesa, Mwanga's father, beheaded one of his wives because she spoke too loudly.

Many of the kingdoms in Uganda developed a feudalistic model in which the ruling class maintained control of cattle, which was the primary form of wealth in those societies. Unlike the feudal systems in Europe, land in Uganda was not the personal possession of the ruling class, but the peasants in Uganda still paid taxes to the ruling class for the crops which the peasants produced. Given this situation, it is not surprising that the commoners in Uganda at times expressed an unfavorable view of the ruling class. One researcher reported a particular exchange in Busoga in which a commoner told a member of the royal clan: "You princes have always been scoundrels!"

Despite the often harsh nature of the rulers in Buganda, Europeans themselves acknowledged that Buganda developed a very sophisticated level of organization. Robert Pickering Ashe wrote that the rulers of Buganda "exacted the most scrupulous modesty on pain even of death." Ashe goes on to note that the people of Buganda wore bark-cloth, for which Buganda was famous for manufacturing. Buganda also exported this bark-cloth as well. The political structure of Buganda was also very complex as well. Buganda was centralized under the rule of the *Kabaka* and each district was overseen by rulers which were appointed by the *Kabaka*.

The ruler of Buganda maintained a permanent armed force, which served as bodyguards. A national army was raised whenever

Buganda was at war, although Buganda's influence in the region was maintained through diplomacy as well as warfare. This was true of the island of Uvuma, which the rulers of Buganda were generally on good terms with. Mutesa broke with this policy when he attempted to conquer the island, but he was defeated by the Bavuma people. After Mwanga came to power he restored Buganda's friendly relationship with the Uvuma.

Bunyoro was also a very well organized kingdom as well. Bunyoro-Kitara was a powerful empire under the rule of the Bachwezi dynasty. The Bachwezi dynasty's power eventually declined and was replaced by the Babito dynasty. Splits within the Babito dynasty led to the creation of new kingdoms. Toro was one of those kingdoms which split from the ruling Babito dynasty in Bunyoro. Babito rulers also established themselves in Busoga as well.

During Kabarega's reign Bunyoro and Toro had a confrontational relationship. Cunningham noted that the Batoro people were raided by the Bunyoro kingdom under Kabarega and for this reason the Batoro people of the Toro kingdom were very grateful for the "advent of peaceful government" which was brought through colonization. The colonialists depicted Kabarega as the aggressor, when in fact his attacks against Toro were actually motivated by self-defense. The Europeans had built forts in Toro and it was from these forts that some African soldiers attacked Bunyoro under the orders of the Europeans and Toro's king, Kasagama. There was also concern on the part of some Europeans that Kabarega could take control of all of Uganda. H.R. Fox Bourne explained that Mwanga's authority "was always weak" and that "had it not been for British intervention, the whole country might before now have fallen under the dominion of Kabarega". Although many of Kabarega's European foes developed a very negative perception of him, he was also described by one European as being "a thoroughly hospitable and intelligent man."

The French also encountered resistance in their colonization campaign. One of the most notable examples of this was Ahmadu Bamba, who was an Islamic religious leader who was arrested and exiled to Gabon in 1895. The French feared that Bamba was plotting a violent uprising against them. Although this was not the case with Bamba, France certainly met violent resistance on the part of other African leaders.

Al Hajj Umar encountered the French around 1846. During the meeting they accepted his "protestations of friendship" and wanted to co-operate with him in building his empire. In the years that followed Umar expanded his empire. He defeated the Mandinka state and then moved towards the Upper Senegal valley in 1854, to combat the "pagan" Bambara state of Karta. To achieve this, he called on the Muslims in Senegal to assist him. It was also during this period of expansion in the 1850s that Umar began recruiting forces to seize control of Senegal from the French. The confrontation between Umar's forces and the French in 1860 was brief, however, since Umar quickly realized that they could not defeat the French. Failing to defeat the French, Umar turned his attention to the east and the Middle Niger. Umar's activities, in a sense, helped to assist French colonization in the region. As was often the case, rather than uniting in the face of European expansion, Umar attempted to subjugate neighboring African people.

Samory Touré, who founded the Wassoulou Empire, was called the "Black Napoleon" by the French because of his military tactics. His war of resistance lasted from 1883 until 1898. Touré established one of the most powerful armies in West Africa. Much of his military success was due to the fact that Touré managed to acquire modern European weapons. He also had blacksmiths who were capable of manufacturing guns. Touré attempted to form an alliance with the British to discourage the French from taking control of his land. When this failed, Touré attempted to negotiate with the French. Touré signed two treaties with France, but he once again waged war on the French when he realized that they were encouraging rebellion in areas that Touré had conquered. Moreover, the French were also preventing Touré from acquiring weapons from Sierra Leone. In 1890, Touré concluded a treaty with the British in Sierra Leone, which allowed him to buy modern weapons for the next three years. Although Touré put up considerable resistance, he was captured by a surprise attack in 1898. Touré was exiled to Gabon where he died in 1900.

Like Samory Touré, Béhanzin of Dahomey also fought the French to maintain the independence of his kingdom. In preparation to defend his kingdom from a potential attack from the French, Béhanzin purchased a number of modern weapons from German firms. The French were making preparations of their own to conquer Dahomey. They placed a mixed race commander named Alfred-Amédée Dodds in charge of the expedition in Dahomey. Dodds marched his soldiers towards Dahomey's capital, Abomey, where he was confronted by Dahomey's forces. In the ensuing battle, Dahomey lost about 2,000 soldiers. Dodds' army also freed Yoruba slaves, who in turn destroyed Dahomey's harvest.

After the battle, Dodds demanded a large indemnity to be paid, as well as for Béhanzin to hand over all of his weapons. Béhanzin refused these terms. Instead, he set Abomey on fire and then fled to the northern part of his kingdom. There Béhanzin regrouped his army and carried out a number of raids against areas that were under French control. The French launched another expedition that was led by Dodds again. The final confrontation took place in 1894. The French successfully conquered northern Dahomey and arrested Béhanzin.

Another location where the French encountered resistance was in the Islamic kingdom of Futa Jallon, in West Africa. The state of Futa Jallon was formed when Fula immigrants declared a *jihad* on the non-Islamic Yalunka people. By 1881, France was attempting to expand their influence in West Africa into Futa Jallon. France attempted to peacefully expand into Futa Jallon through negotiations at first, but these attempts were rejected by the Fulas. The first sign of resistance by the Fulas was when they rejected the French interpretation of a treaty that was made in July 1881. The Fulas had no intention of accepting a French protectorate. Ibrahim Sori made this clear when he told the French envoy Jean Bayol that: "Futa must remain in the possession of the Fulas and France to the French." A new treaty was formed in May 1893, but the Fulas remained opposed to France's goals.

The Fulas had a policy of supporting African resistance against the French. This included giving their support to Samory Touré. They provided Samory with guns and bullocks in exchange for gold, rubber, and slaves. They also allowed him to use Futa Jallon as a base to further launch attacks against the French. The French were aware that the Fulas had been arming Samory, although the

Fulas denied this. The Fulas also worked to exploit differences between European colonial powers to their advantage. For instance, Bokar Biro made a promise of submission to France, while at the same time making an offer to surrender to the British. The British declined the offer, however.

Although the British were not interested in taking control over Futa Jallon, the Fulas maintained close relations with the government of Sierra Leone, which was a British colony at the time. The Fulas used this close relationship to Sierra Leone to trick France into thinking that the British were an obstacle to the relationship between Futa Jallon and France. In 1894 and 1895, Bokar Biro promised France that he would travel to Conakry to finalize a treaty in which Futa would accept French sovereignty. Biro failed to do so, however, and explained that the instigation of authorities in Sierra Leone were the reason for this. In June 1895, the British government ceased official relations with Futa Jallon. Despite this, Bokar Biro would still use the potential threat of seeking British assistance to prolong finalizing the protectorate treaty with France.

The initial stages of Fula resistance to French expansion in Futa Jallon was not one of armed resistance, but rather simply attempting to prolong having to conclude a treaty with France which would have given France authority over the region. Between 1894 and 1896, Bokar Biro had given a number of excuses for why he could not finalize a treaty with France. The governor decided that rather than waiting for Bokar to come to Conakry, he would send one of his administrators to deal with Bokar directly. Bokar was presented with a treaty, which he apparently signed. The French administration would later learn that Bokar did not actually sign the treaty, but had written an Arabic expression which meant "in the name of the gracious and merciful God." Bokar also included a note in Arabic, which stated that Bokar would not give a definitive answer until he spoke with the council of elders. Bokar had once again avoided concluding a treaty with France. This action by Bokar not only caused him to lose the French support that he once had, but France also decided to use military force to bring Futa Jallon under their control.

One of the disadvantages that Futa Jallon faced was that it was not a completely united state. The Alimami, who was the ruler of the state, ruled over a central government, but there were provincial chiefs that enjoyed a degree of autonomy. For instance, if the Alimami went to war, local chiefs sometimes refused to support that war. Chiefs typically demonstrated their loyalty to the central government through sending tributes and gifts to the Alimami. The chief of the Labe province was especially noted for demonstrating a large degree of independence from the Alimami. Labe was the largest and richest province in Futa Jallon.

Bokar Biro's rule helped to further disunite Futa Jallon. After the death of Ibrahim Sori, Bokar came to power after assassinating his elder brother, Mamadu Pate. Once in power, Bokar attempted to strengthen the central authority of the government by checking the independent behavior of local chiefs by deposing recalcitrant chiefs. Bokar's policies troubled many of the local chiefs, including Alfa Yaya of Labe, whose goal was to rule over an independent kingdom of Labe. Bokar waged war on Yaya to punish him for wanting to make Labe an independent nation. Bokar's troops were defeated by a coalition of forces by Yaya and another chief known as Alfa Ibrahima. Alfa Ibrahima was the chief of Fugumba. He assisted Bokar in 1890 during the war of succession to the throne and was responsible for Bokar's victory. Ibrahima would later be disappointed by Bokar's conduct once Bokar became the ruler of Futa Jallon.

Bokar's assault against Yaya was only the second instance of war between the central government and a local chief in the history of Futa Jallon, but it came at a very unfortunate time. The defeat of Bokar destabilized Futa Jallon. Bokar was forced to flee. He managed to regain control of Futa Jallon in 1896 with assistance from the French administration in Guinea. Bokar had once again deceived the French. In order to get the French to support his efforts to regain control in Futa Jallon, Bokar had made promises to the French administration which he did not intend to keep. Bokar had effectively alienated the support of both the local chiefs in Futa Jallon and the French administration in Guinea.

Bokar had also managed to alienate the masses, who were growing frustrated with his complete disregard for their property. Bokar engaged in pillages in Futa Jallon. He also freely allowed his sons and nephews to plunder the possessions of his subjects. Some Fulas fled the region to escape these abuses. Others believed that they would be better off with French masters ruling them instead. The French themselves had hoped to win the support of the masses in their attempt to take control of Futa Jallon.

At a time when France was attempting to expand in West Africa and to bring Futa Jallon under its control, the last thing that needed to happen was disunity within Futa Jallon, but this is precisely what Bokar had helped to create. The local chiefs were now willing to side with the French against Bokar. Alfa Yaya attempted to use the French to help him establish the independence of Labe. Alfa Ibrahima, however, continued to oppose both Bokar and France. Ibrahima's goal was the removal of Bokar in favor of a more capable ruler. By 1896, France had identified six of the thirteen local chiefs as being pro-French. France implemented divide and rule tactics to achieve their goals in Futa Jallon.

In August 1896, Bokar's term as Alimami was over, but he refused to give up his power to Omaru Bademba, who was the candidate that was favored by the electoral council and provincial chiefs. This demonstrated the extent of Bokar's authoritarian practices and provided a pretext for French intervention. They planned to install the pro-French Bademba as the Alimami. This mission was carried out successfully, and Bademba was installed at Timbo, Futa Jallon's capital. Bokar quickly worked to organize resistance to expel the French. This included reaching out to Alfa Yaya, Alfa Ibrahima, and other former enemies for support. Although Bokar had helped to disunite Futa Jallon, he was now urging for unity in order to repel the French. Some of the chiefs gave Bokar promises of commitment, but had no real intentions of supporting him. Yaya and Ibrahima outright rejected his offer.

Bokar suffered his final defeat on November 14, 1896. His soldiers were defeated by a small French platoon, which was supported by Omaru Bademba and Alfa Ibrahima. Bokar was captured and killed by Bademba's warriors. Bokar's death ended the Fula resistance to French expansion. Bokar's forces were at a major technological disadvantage, as they were armed with muskets, whereas their enemies were armed with tirailleurs, which had much better range. Moreover, Bokar's policies proved to be divisive. Many Africans turned to the French simply out of their hatred for Bokar. The French skillfully exploited these internal differences.

All across Africa, Africans fought and resisted European colonization, but Africans proved to be no match for the military might of the European colonialists. Countless Africans were killed in the wars of colonization. Not only were African warriors killed in these wars, but civilians were targeted as well. In their attempts to subjugate Africans, Europeans often resorted to burning and pillaging villages.

One of the pretenses of colonialism was to stamp out the slave trade. Among those championing the cause of ending slavery in Africa was Leopold. Despite his rhetoric about ending slavery in the Congo, Leopold oversaw what was perhaps the worst use of slave labor seen in colonial Africa. Tippu Tip, a wealthy slave trader in East Africa, sold thousands of slaves to Leopold. In return for being "liberated," these former slaves were required to work for the Force Publique for seven years. Leopold later parted ways with Tippu Tip and turned his attention towards a campaign against the Arab slave traders, though after this campaign many slave traders were placed in positions as state officials.

Leopold's looting of the Congo devastated and disrupted many societies. An American named Edgar Canisius recorded the story that was told to him by a Congolese woman named Ilanga. She described life in her country before the coming of the Belgians:

> Our village is called Waniendo, after our chief Niendo...It is a large village near a small stream, and surrounded by large fields of *mohago* (cassava) and *muhindu* (maize) and other foods, for we all worked hard at our plantations, and always had plenty to eat...We never had war in our country, and the men had not many arms except knives...

Ilanga recalled being captured along with her husband Oleka and her sister Katinga. Ilanga described: "We were dragged into the road, and were tied together with cords about our necks, so that we could not escape. We were all crying, for now we knew that we were to be taken as slaves. The soldiers beat us with iron sticks from their guns [...]."

They were made to march. Ilanga's sister had her baby in her arms so she was not made to carry a basket, but Oleka was made to carry a goat. After five days of marching, the soldiers threw

Katinga's baby into the grass and left it to die. They made her carry cooking pots. Ilanga's husband became weak from lack of food and could continue no longer. The soldiers beat him and then stabbed him with "the long knives they put on the ends of their guns." Ilanga said: "I saw the blood spurt out, and then saw him no more, for we passed over the brow of a hill and he was out of sight." Many young men were killed the same way and many babies were thrown into the grass on the way to "the white men's town at Nyangwe."

The situation was so harsh for the Congolese that they sang:

> We are tired of living under this tyranny.
>
> We cannot endure that our women and children are taken away
>
> And dealt with by white savages.
>
> We shall make war...
>
> We know that we shall die, but we want to die.

In colonial Kenya a number of abuses occurred on the part of the ruling British colonial government. Waiyaki wa Hinga was one of the victims of those abuses. After the British broke a peace treaty that he had agreed to, Waiyaki launched an attack on Fort Smith. Waiyaki harassed the British forces until they finally captured him and decided to bury him alive, head first.

Captain Richard Meinertzhagen of the King's African Rifles gave the following description of an expedition he engaged in while serving in Kenya:

> I have performed a most unpleasant duty today. I made a night march to the village at the edge of the forest where the white settler had been so brutally murdered the day before yesterday. The war drums were sounding throughout the night we reached the village without incident and surrounded it. By the light of fires we could see savages dancing in the village, and

our guides assured me that they were dancing round the mutilated body of the white man.

I gave orders that every living thing except children should be killed without mercy. I hated the work and was anxious to get through with it [...] Every soul was either shot or bayoneted, and I am happy to say that no children were in the village. [...] We burned all the huts and razed the banana plantations to the ground.

In 2012, Wambuga Wa Nyingi, Jane Muthoni Mara, and Paulo Muoka Nzili were granted the right to sue the British government over the mistreatment that they endured during the colonial period. They suffered beatings, tortures, rape, and castration. All the documents concerning these abuses were concealed for decades before coming to light. These papers showed that suspected rebels were beaten to death, burned alive, castrated, and kept in manacles. Prior to the release of these papers, it was no secret that suspected Mau Mau rebels were used for labor. The Embakasi airport in Nairobi was built from the labor of Mau Mau suspects.

Much of the abuses that went on in Kenya under the colonial administration were purposely kept quiet. Ministers and senior civil servants in London knew about these abuses, but publicly denied that they were happening. Eric Griffith-Jones, the attorney general of the British administration in Kenya, stated that in order to keep the abuses legal, the suspects "must be beaten mainly on their upper body," and that vulnerable parts of the body like the spleen, liver, and kidneys must be avoided. According to Griffith-Jones, if the colonial government was going to sin, they "must sin quietly."

Such violence was also a frequent occurrence in colonial Nigeria. There was an incident in which the Egba United Government, which was an independent African government within the colony of Nigeria, ordered the arrest of a 90 year old named Sobiyi Ponlade because he refused to order his people to participate in the unpaid labor program that was meant to build and repair roads in the area. Ponlade remained defiant and when the Egba government tried to arrest Ponlade, the old man resisted. The police roughed him up and dragged him into court. There he was publicly humiliated, beaten, and tied to a tree all night. A British commissioner named P.V. Young defended tying Ponlade to a tree as a means to prevent him from committing suicide. Ponlade's poor treatment outraged those that opposed the Egba government. A few days later Ponlade died in prison and few believed the official report that he had died of natural causes.

Ponlade's death incited outrage towards the Egba government and the ruling *Alake*. The *Alake* requested that British Commissioner Young arrest the Ogboni chiefs from the Ijemo, including the high-ranking oluwo chief. The *Alake* was warned that British intervention could put the autonomy of Egba at risk, but the *Alake*, who was desperate to maintain control of his throne, wanted the British assistance. The Ogboni was a sort of religious and political organization among the Yoruba people. The *Alake* attempted to bribe the Ogboni for support, but they sided against him.

Riots broke out on August 5, 1914. After three days of trying, the *Alake* was unable to quell the rioting. He turned to colonial officers to end the rioting, which opened the possibility of the British terminating their 1893 treaty and completely taking control of Abeokuta. The colonial troops moved into Abeokuta and the treaty was terminated, ending Egba's independence. The British reasoned that "if the head of state says publicly that he is compelled to appeal for the assistance of armed forces of the colonial government, the state can no longer be deemed capable of standing alone as an independent state." With the Egba government now incorporated into the colonial government, Commissioner D.E. Wilson was sent to put down the uprising.

The uprising was put down with brutal force. The oluwo was under the impression that Wilson was coming for peaceful talks. When Wilson and his army arrived, they encountered over one thousand unarmed people who wanted to talk. Wilson asked the people to hand over their chiefs, but no one obeyed these commands. According to Wilson's account, someone in the unarmed crowd tried to kill him and was shot. Within the span of a few minutes, the oluwo, two of the oluwo's wives, and more than thirty other people had been killed by the British officers. This incident was presented as an act of self-defense on the part of the British officers, but this was not the case at all. After having killed the oluwo, Wilson then ordered his soldiers to enter the oluwo's house where they killed his two wives and a young boy. The crowd was dispersed by force and following this dispersal the colonial troops destroyed houses and other property in the city. In the aftermath of the death and destruction, Commissioner Young claimed that the *Alake* had instructed them to use violent force to teach the people obedience towards the king.

In the Gold Coast, the British used the guise of civilizing the Asante people as a justification for their attempts to bring the Asante kingdom under British rule. The Gold Coast born nationalist and writer Joseph Casely Hayford highlighted the hypocrisy of Britain's claims to be conquering the Asante people in the hopes of civilizing them:

> For, mark you, the talk about human sacrifices and barbarous customs and slave-raiding is all cant. What lies behind it all is the desire for the good things of Ashanti that would come into the pockets of the British capitalist. How many thousands are mowed down by the Maxim in a single expedition? And in times of peace are not "rebel chiefs" freely hanged?

Given the brutalities that Africans had to endure it is no surprise that there were frequent struggles against colonization. Some examples of rebellion and resistance to colonialism were previously mentioned before, but that topic will be expanded on so that one can get an idea of just how widespread rebellion and resistance was on the part of Africans. In Sierra Leone there was a railroad strike in 1919 and another in 1926. In February 1931, hundreds of Africans led an armed revolt against the colonial government. Under the leadership of a Muslim named Hahilara these rebels invaded the Kambia district. He encouraged Africans to refuse to pay taxes and to drive out British officials. He also demanded land for the landless peasants. The colonial government finally managed to kill Hahilara after a bloody conflict that also cost the life of Captain H.J. Holmes, who commanded the British troops.

In Kenya, Harry Thuku protested the high taxes and the forced labor of the colonial regime. His movement spread rapidly which concerned the government. They ordered the King's African Rifles to suppress the growing movement and persuaded chiefs to sign a proclamation which appealed for the masses to return to work with the promise that the government would reduce taxation and increase wages. Thuku was subsequently arrested, which caused a large strike and crowds demanded Thuku's release. Soldiers were ordered to fire at the crowds and more than 150 were killed. Thuku was later shipped to Kismay, which was on the Somali border.

Thuku's protests were the forerunner for the even more radical methods of the Mau Mau, who violently attacked both Europeans and Africans that supported the British regime. This movement was led by Dedan Kimathi and Waruhiu Itote. The goal of this movement was self-government, and Kimathi himself was reported to have stated: "I do not lead rebels but I lead Africans who want their self-government and land. My people want to live in a better world than they met with when they were born."

An African named John Chilembwe led a revolt in Nyasaland in 1915. Chilembwe was educated in America as a minister. This would profoundly shape Chilembwe's views on racism and colonialism. Chilembwe was a student in America at the time of the race riots in Wilmington, North Carolina in 1898. Reverend Charles S. Morris, who was an eyewitness to the events at Wilmington, journeyed with Chilembwe back to Africa. After Chilembwe's revolt was put down the colonial government alleged that radical literature from African Americans was one of the factors that motivated the uprising.

After being educated in America, Chilembwe returned to Nyasaland where he established a church of his own. This church was assisted by some African Americans that Chilembwe managed to recruit in America. In Nyasaland, Chilembwe grew frustrated with the mistreatment of African people by the colonialists. He was especially outraged that Africans were being recruited to fight in World War I, which resulted in a large number of them being killed. In November 1914, Chilembwe wrote a letter to the *Nyasaland Times*, which was censored. In this letter he complained that "we have been invited to shed our innocent blood in this world's war...we are imposed upon more than any other nationality under the sun." Chilembwe was himself mistreated by both the white planters and the white missionaries. This, along with his reading about the Hebrews of the Old Testament, inspired

Chilembwe to revolt. This uprising was supported by the estate workers. Together they killed the five European heads of the estate, sparing their wives and children.

The revolt was short-lived. Chilembwe had delivered a sermon in a church, where the estate manager's head was displayed on the pulpit. Afterwards the police and soldiers were sent to capture him and the other rebels. The rebels attempted to flee, but were hunted down. Twenty of the captured rebels were hanged, with Chilembwe himself being shot down and killed. This revolt in particular was of major concern to the European colonists, as one writer explained:

> While their countrymen in Europe fought the bloodiest war ever known, in Africa Europeans were instinctively white men first—and German and British second, [for] John Chilembwe was part of something that in the end would swamp all their colonial dreams.

Chilembwe was not the only one to revolt during World War I. The Giriama people of Kenya used the war as an opportunity to revolt in 1914. The British had a number of conflicts with them prior to 1914 because the Giriama refused to be moved from their land. They also resisted attempts made by Europeans to take away their young men to work on European controlled farms. The 1914 revolt was the largest conflict between the two. The British responded to this revolt by burning down houses and seizing the property of the Giriama. The Giriama resorted to guerilla warfare, but were eventually defeated.

There was a revolt in the French Congo in 1924. This revolt only lasted several days before the French suppressed it. In 1928 there was an even larger revolt. This revolt lasted four months and the natives managed to inflict a number of defeats on the French. In an attempt to suppress the revolts, the French shot suspects and publicly whipped old men and women. This did little to suppress dissent, as the Africans were rebelling again by April 1930. In 1929 there was a famine in Rwanda, which was then under the control of the Belgians. The Africans in Rwanda revolted. This revolt spread to British Uganda. Among the leaders of the revolt was the daughter of the king of Rwanda.

The Devastation and Economics of the African Holocaust

The European excursion into Africa was violent and destructive, and did little to contribute to the civilizing of the "savage" population. In fact, the European concept of civilizing Africa began with the notion that Africans were a backward people and needed civilizing, which was certainly not the case at all. One field that we can look at is the medical field because it is without doubt that European knowledge did improve Africa in this regard, to a limited extent, yet this has also been problematic for a number of reasons.

Contrary to the popular belief spread by the European colonialists, Africans did in fact have real medical knowledge. In the United States, Cotton Mather helped battle a smallpox outbreak by using a method for smallpox inoculation that he had learned from his slave Onesimus. This method was a common practice in the part of Africa where Onesimus came from. Onesimus was himself inoculated before being enslaved. A clergyman named Benjamin Coleman was interviewing slaves in Boston and he also heard stories of this inoculation method. Mather was willing to try this technique, although others opposed it. In the end, out of about 300 people who were inoculated, only five or six died.

Not only did this European civilizing mission deny that Africans had their own medical knowledge before colonization, but whatever medical benefits that Africa received during colonization was not enjoyed by the majority of the population. The Portuguese controlled their colonies for 500 years, and despite claiming that they were on a civilizing mission, in Mozambique they did not train a single African doctor. This was actually a step backwards for Mozambique's medical development as Gungunhana, the Nguni ruler in Mozambique, had previously requested for a Swiss doctor and kept that doctor in his court. Concerning medical treatment, Angola was not in much better shape than Mozambique and both of those two colonies received more attention from the Portuguese colonial administration than did Guinea-Bissau.

The Ridge hospital in the Gold Coast was reserved for whites, with few exceptions. Korle Bu, which was the principal hospital in Accra, the capital of the Gold Coast, was overcrowded and Korle Bu was considered to be one of the best hospitals in Africa. In Ibadan, Nigeria, the British had segregated hospitals, and, of course, the European hospitals were the ones that provided the better treatment. The African hospitals were also very scarce in relation to the total population of Africans. The Tuberculosis Commission of 1912 reported on the hospitals in South Africa, stating:

> Hospital services are so inadequate that incurable tuberculosis and other cases are simply sent home to die— and spread the infection. In some areas, a single doctor has to attend to the needs of 40,000 people.

The poor medical conditions that the Africans endured was also made worse by the strenuous labor that they were forced to perform to benefit the colonial governments. In South Africa the Africans were forced to work the mines, a job which takes a serious toll on the health of the worker. In 1930, scurvy along with other epidemics broke out in Tanganyika and killed hundreds of workers. These same workers were not even paid enough to afford a proper diet. The mission to bring civilization to Africa failed to bring adequate medical advancements to a good portion of the population in Africa, especially the laborers who needed medical facilities the most.

This neglect for the medical needs of the Africans was simply a larger part of the overall neglect of African people on the part of the European colonists. Of the French colonies, Chad was among the more neglected. For France, Chad was the source of raw cotton and labor, but France paid little attention to Chad's development. France did little to unify the territory and was very slow in the process of modernizing Chad. A country study of Chad described the colonial administration as follows:

> Although France had put forth considerable effort during the conquest of Chad, the ensuing administration of the territory was halfhearted. Officials in the French colonial service resisted assignments to Chad, so posts often went to novices or to out-of-favor officials. One historian of France's empire has concluded that it was almost impossible to be too demented or depraved to be

considered unfit for duty in Chad. Still, major scandals occurred periodically, and many of the posts remained vacant. In 1928, for example, 42 percent of the Chadian subdivisions lacked official administrators.

The supposed civilizing mission also failed to bring adequate education to Africa. In Tanzania, Julius Nyerere pointed out that "despite the Education and Health services provided by some Christian Missionaries and later begun by colonial governments, at independence less than 50%, of Tanzanians children went to school- and then for only four years or less; 85%, of its adults were illiterate in any language. The country had only 2 African Engineers, 12 Doctors, and perhaps 30 Arts graduates, I was one of them." He also noted that countries such as Congo, Mozambique, Chad, and Somalia were even worse off than Tanzania in that regard.

Yet another justification for colonization was this idea that the colonists were somehow suppressing the violent tribal urges of the Africans. This has not been the case, however. In fact, European colonization helped to fuel many of these conflicts through the usage of divide and conquer tactics. For example, in South Africa the Bantu Education Act of 1953 promoted differences between the various ethnic groups, including the Zulus, Xhosa, and Sotho. European colonization made tribal tensions worse through the usage of divide and conquer tactics, and the result has often been tribal conflicts and wars, such as the civil war in Nigeria and the genocide in Rwanda.

The final aspect of European colonization that must be addressed is the lingering political and economic impact of colonialism. Although African nations became independent, the colonial regimes were largely replaced with African leaders that were subservient to the interests of the former colonial powers. This was in a sense done by design. The education of the colonial regime was meant to produce Africans that were subservient and loyal to their colonial masters. Even though the education was meant to serve the interests of the colonialists, this education was restricted to a very small number of Africans.

Concerning education, the Belgians believed that the Africans should be gradually civilized. For this reason, it was nearly impossible for the people of the Congo and Rwanda-Burundi to receive anything above primary education. The Belgians even argued that a highly educated African would not be able to serve his own people. It was not until 1948 that the Belgians established secondary schools in their colonies. By the time that Congo became independent the nation only had 16 graduates. Things were not much different in Southern Rhodesia where in 1954 only 16.5 percent of African children were in school.

There were many barriers to education for Africans in Northern Rhodesia. To begin with, the colonialists argued that since Africans did not pay as much tax per head as the Europeans did then the Africans should not be given the same education that the European settlers enjoyed. Despite the fact that the wealth that was produced in Northern Rhodesia was due to African labor, in 1959 the British Colonial Office stated that they did not have enough money to build schools to provide primary education for all children. In 1960, only 43 percent of African children were in school in Northern Rhodesia and only 1 percent of those children received a secondary school education.

Another feature of this colonial educational system was its unevenness. Those Africans who lived in areas that produced more wealth for the Europeans also received more educational opportunities. For example, in Gambia literacy was high in the Bathurst town, but was low outside of that town. In Uganda most of the education was centered in Buganda and in the Gold Coast the southern territories received better education than the north. Kwame Nkrumah complained:

> When my colleagues and I came into office in 1951, we found some government schools in the principal towns of the country. But they served only a small part of the urban populations and a minute section of the rural areas. The villages, where most of our people live, boasted few schools; such as there were, were operated mainly by the missions. The number of secondary schools was limited, being based mainly in Cape Coast. These, too, were largely the products of missionary endeavour.

In the system of colonialism, education also meant little in terms of obtaining a job. An African could be more skilled and educated than a European in a certain profession, yet the European, by virtue of his race, would be given the higher position and thus get paid more. This is the point Amilcar Cabral made when he stated:

> I was an agronomist working under a European who everybody knew was one of the biggest idiots in Guinea; I could have taught him his job with my eyes shut but he was the boss: this is something which counts a lot, this is the confrontation which really matters.

Amilcar Cabral was himself from the assimilado class. He was educated in Portugal and even married a Portuguese woman there. He would later go on to become one of the foremost leaders in the African struggle against colonialism. For his anti-colonial activities, Cabral was assassinated in 1973.

The colonial education produced a class of confused Africans. This is why Blaise Diagne, a native of Senegal, could proclaim, "I am a Frenchman first, and a Negro African second." He was so beholden to the French that when a French newspaper reported that W.E.B. Du Bois was a disciple of Marcus Garvey, though the two were bitter rivals, Diagne could not go to the Third Pan-African Congress because he did not want to participate in a congress with an associate of Garvey. Diagne feared the fact that Garvey was preaching, "Back to Africa and kick the white man out."

Kofi Busia, who served as Prime Minister for Ghana, is another example of an African who was miseducated. He gave the following description of his days of going to school in the British colonial system:

> At the end of my first year at secondary school (Mfantsipim, Cape Coast, Ghana), I went home to Wenchi for the Christmas vacation. I had not been home for four years, and on that visit, I became painfully aware of my isolation. I understood our community far less than the boys of my own age who had never been to school. Over the years, as I went through college and university, I felt increasingly that the education I received taught me more and more about Europe and less and less

about my own society.

Julius Nyerere pointed out:

> In practice, colonialism, with its implications of racial superiority, was replaced by a combination of neo-colonialism and government by local elites who too often had learned to despise their own African traditions and the mass of the people who worked on the land. External control of African economies continued, usually by the former colonial power.

As far as the French were concerned education was only required for a select number of Africans—those Africans that could help France's imperial interests. Walter Rodney points out:

> Indeed, the French concentrated on selecting a small minority, who would be thoroughly subjected to French cultural imperialism, and who would aid France in administering its vast African colonial possessions. William Ponty, an early Governor-General of French West Africa, spoke in terms of forming "an elite of young people destined to aid our own efforts."

Education and missionary work were important aspects of maintaining colonial control in Africa. At the same time attempts by African people to organize schools of their own was seen as a potential threat to the colonial regime. The British shut down the 149 schools of the Kikuyu Independent Schools Association as well as other independent schools because they were seen as "training grounds for rebellion" during the Mau Mau uprising. Under the Salazar regime in Portugal, some Africans who were educated in Portugal were banned from returning home because they had been introduced to progressive ideas. It was clear then that the purpose of the education that was given to the African was not to empower the African, but to make the African a better servant, and when that education seemed like it was empowering the African or encouraging the African to rebel then it had to be shut down.

Based on this information we see that European education succeeded in creating a class of European-minded Africans that served the interests of the former colonizers. Many of these same European-minded Africans would assume the leadership of the post-colonial African states, and as such they essentially maintained European control over their nations. This was apparent in Senegal under the presidency of Léopold Senghor. Eric Williams, the prime minister of Trinidad and Tobago, visited Senegal and described the nation as being "tied hand and foot to France, and nobody attempts to conceal it."

It was this same class of leadership in Africa that oversaw neo-colonialism or the continuation of Western dominance over the economic lives of African people. In effect, African nations were given political independence, but the economies of African nations were essentially under the control of the West. This lack of control for Africa also included abuses along the lines of what occurred during the colonial period. Therefore, even after gaining independence, the West continued to profit from Africa's suffering. The sale of blood diamonds is a well-known example of Western exploitation of Africa's suffering. As mentioned before, diamonds were a major aspect of the wealth that Europeans acquired from their exploitation of Africa. Rebels in a number of civil wars in Africa were able to use diamond sales to finance their violent activities. Nations such as Liberia, Sierra Leone, Congo, and Angola were especially devastated by these diamond funded wars throughout the 1990s.

Ibrahim Fofana was one of the victims of the war in Sierra Leone. Rebels attacked his village, capturing him and others. Ibrahim was locked in a house with about 53 other people. The rebels then set the house on fire. Ibrahim managed to escape the fire, but he did not escape from the experience uninjured. The rebels cut off both of his hands. Ibrahim later learned that his wife and children were burned alive when their house was set on fire. Years after the war Ibrahim lamented that if not for the blood diamonds, the war would have ended much earlier than it did.

The corruption and incompetence of the government in Sierra Leone was one of the major factors leading to the civil war. The diamond industry, especially, was exploited by government officials that personally profited from diamond sales. As government officials enriched themselves, Sierra Leone became impoverished and infrastructure collapsed. The collapse of Sierra Leone led to the rise of radical government critics. Among these critics was Foday Sankoh, the founder of the Revolutionary United Front (RUF). Sankoh also allied himself with Charles Taylor in Liberia, who assisted the RUF.

The RUF built up an army to challenge the government. To build this army the RUF took advantage of the large number of uneducated and impoverished young men in Sierra Leone that were frustrated with the government. In 1991, the RUF struck and within a year the government of Sierra Leone was overthrown by a military coup. The RUF continued its war, however. The change of government mattered little to Sankoh who wanted power for himself.

The RUF captured people and forced them to mine diamonds at gunpoint. The workers were barely fed and those who attempted to rest were killed. Those who were suspected of having taken any of the diamonds that they found were also killed. These diamonds were smuggled out of the country and the revenue from the diamond sales were used to buy weapons such as AK-47s. Many atrocities were committed throughout the war. Villages were raided and destroyed. The murder, mutilation, and rape of civilians became commonplace. Following the election of Ahmad Tejan Kabbah in 1996, the brutalities of the RUF increased. The RUF began to amputate the hands of many of their victims as a symbolic act of punishment towards those who voted for Tejan Kabbah. The RUF often asked their victims if they wanted short-sleeves or long-sleeves, which was their way of asking their victims if they wanted their arm chopped off at the wrist or at the elbow.

Sexual violence against women by RUF soldiers was commonplace. A woman named Musu Farrow recalled being raped by RUF rebels. Kumba Mbindie described an even more gruesome experience. Her family attempted to escape the rebels, but to no avail. The rebels caught up with them and dragged her husband into the jungle where they cut his hands off. One of the rebels used a stick to forcibly abort Mbindie's unborn child.

Children were also caught up in the conflict. Many children were maimed and killed, while others did the maiming and killing.

This included both boys and girls. Girls were used as both soldiers and sexual slaves. One girl named Lovette Freeman was captured and sexually abused by the rebels at the age of 14. She would later become one of their soldiers. In one instance, she accompanied the rebels in looting a house. Freeman held both a woman and her baby at gunpoint.

Following the overthrow of Kabbah by soldiers of the Sierra Leonean army the RUF was invited into the capital city of Freetown. The rebels plundered the city, harassing and robbing civilians. The rebels were eventually driven out of Freetown by the Economic Community of West African States Monitoring Group (ECOMOG), which was a Nigerian led multinational army. They drove the rebels from Freetown and reinstated Kabbah. As the rebels retreated from the city, they destroyed everything that was in their path, including massacring large numbers of civilians.

The rebels made their way back into Freetown where they continued their rampage against the civilian population. ECOMOG once again confronted the rebels, but many civilians were caught in the crossfire as ECOMOG was sometimes unable to distinguish between the rebels and the civilians. Freetown became a warzone and by the time that the rebels were driven out of the capital, thousands of people had been killed.

The civil war in Sierra Leone finally came to an end in 2002 following the signing of a peace agreement, known as the Lomé Peace Accord. This peace agreement ended the war, but there were many setbacks to the agreement. It pardoned the rebels and made Foday Sankoh the vice president of the nation. In this regard Sankoh had achieved his goal. As Vice President he was placed in charge of Sierra Leone's diamond fields. The RUF also continued to hold control of the diamond fields. Sankoh was eventually arrested, but died before he could face trial.

It was revealed that Liberian president Charles Taylor had been involved in the sale of blood diamonds. Liberia would smuggle conflict diamonds out of Sierra Leone and to distribute them to diamond buyers in Europe. Officially the diamonds were recorded as coming out of Liberia, regardless of where the diamonds truly came from. Taylor was later arrested and indicted for his crimes.

Aside from the element of blood diamonds, there was also a political aspect to the civil war in Angola. The war in Angola played directly into the Cold War conflict that was going on at the time, with both the United States and the Soviet Union backing different sides of the conflict. America supported Jonas Savimbi. Savimbi was a rebel in Angola who waged a war against the Portuguese colonizers and then later clashed with the Popular Movement for the Liberation of Angola (MPLA) during the decolonization period and after Angolan independence. The resulting civil war took the lives of more than one million people. The war also injured and maimed countless others. Jonas Savimbi was generally seen as a terrorist by Africans. When he died the Namibian government stated: "Savimbi chose the way of terrorism and turned Angola into a land of many killing fields." Angolans took to the streets to celebrate his death.

While Savimbi may have been seen as a terrorist by most Africans, for much of his military campaign against the MPLA, Savimbi was viewed as an ally by the United States. Ronald Reagan invited Savimbi to the White House and praised him as a "freedom fighter." Reagan and others on the right-wing saw Savimbi as a man who was fighting to liberate Angola from the domination of the socialist MPLA, which was led by José Eduardo dos Santos.

Savimbi was an opportunist who initially wanted a leadership position in the MPLA. Failing to gain the position that he wanted, Savimbi joined a separate anti-colonial group. He joined the Union of Peoples of Angola (UPA), which was led by Holden Roberto, but he later left the UPA because he felt that Roberto was an American stooge. Savimbi then created the National Union for the Total Independence of Angola (UNITA). This group was trained and supplied by China.

Despite Savimbi portraying himself as a revolutionary who was seeking to free Angola from the Portuguese, evidence suggests that he allied himself with the Portuguese colonial government and their secret police. Savimbi even supplied information about rival movements to the Portuguese and engaged in military action against these movements. When the Portuguese left Angola in 1974, Savimbi opted to engage in guerilla warfare against the government rather than take part in the 1975 nationwide elections.

Although Savimbi claimed to be a Maoist when the Chinese were funding his liberation movement, Savimbi quickly became a capitalist and was being financed by the Central Intelligence Agency (CIA) to oppose the Soviet backed MPLA, despite the fact that Savimbi had previously criticized Roberto for being a stooge for the American imperialists. Savimbi received millions of dollars in aid from both Ronald Reagan and George H. Bush. Not only was the United States backing Savimbi and providing support for UNITA, but so was South Africa. South Africa also sent their own troops into Angola and launched air strikes. The only two nations in the world that did not recognize Angola's MPLA government were the United States and South Africa. The Organization of African Unity (OAU) warned that because Savimbi was an agent of the apartheid regime of South Africa who had been involved in the wanton killings of civilians, any American involvement in Angola's affairs would be considered a hostile action against the OAU. Even American officials, such as Richard Moose and Wayne Smith, warned against the United States supporting South Africa. Moose had suspicions that Savimbi, who was educated as a Marxist and trained by Maoists, was still a communist.

The civil war was terribly costly to Angola and caused massive amounts of civilian casualties, as UNITA would indiscriminately target civilians in their attempt to strike terror into the population. It is estimated that more than 300,000 children alone were killed during the conflict. By the 1990s, the Cold War had ended and likewise so did the war in Angola. There was a brief ceasefire in 1991 followed by elections in 1992. After the MPLA won the elections, Savimbi decided to go back to warring with the government.

The newly elected Clinton administration hesitated to recognize the MPLA, hoping that this would pressure the MPLA to give UNITA a greater share in the power. The United States not only failed to recognize the election results and the MPLA, they also failed to denounce UNITA for its violence. The United States finally withdrew their support from Savimbi in 1993 when the Clinton administration finally recognized the government of president Santos. This prompted Savimbi to turn to selling diamonds in return for weapons. UNITA would capture people and force them to mine diamonds under slavery like conditions, similarly to what was done in Sierra Leone. Amputations also became a frequent occurrence in Angola. Savimbi continued his rebellion against the government until his death in 2002.

Diamonds have also played a significant role in the development of Botswana. Botswana has often been cited as the model nation for other African nations given its relative political stability and economic strength, but in many ways Botswana is the classic example of a neo-colonial state. Although Botswana has fared much better than most African nations following independence, Botswana has still been plagued by severe poverty and wealth inequality.

For much of Ian Khama's presidency Botswana has had the distinction of being known as Africa's least corrupt nation. Botswana's history of political stability bears that out. Since Botswana received its independence in 1966, Botswana has not experienced a civil war or a coup. Botswana was once the British Protectorate of Bechuanaland, established in 1885 at the request of Khama III to avoid having his land being conquered by the Boers. Setshele I had previously attempted to make the same request to the British after he defeated the Boers at the Battle of Dimawe in 1852. The nation's first president was Sir Seretse Khama, a British educated African who was knighted by the queen in 1966.

Under Khama's presidency, Botswana's economy became a thriving one, largely due to Botswana's diamond supply. Khama's rule also proved to be a controversial one for neighboring South Africa. Seretse Khama had married a white woman, causing the South African government to pressure Britain into forcing Khama into exile from the then British protectorate. A few years later Khama was allowed to return to Bechuanaland where he would eventually found the Botswana Democratic Party and lead Botswana into independence. The Botswana Democratic Party would continue to dominate the politics of Botswana following independence.

Despite the outward appearance of economic and political stability, as well as a lack of corruption, Botswana has faced serious problems concerning inequality and human rights abuses. The most obvious example of this is the tensions between the San people and the ruling elite from the Tswana tribe. The San people have been battling eviction from their own homeland due to the fact that their homeland has diamond deposits. In 2006, the San people actually won a court case, which ruled that they were illegally removed from their land and had a right to return. This did not end the persecution of the San people, however. Despite Botswana's "democracy," many ethnic groups remained marginalized and left out of the decision making process.

Moreover, Botswana has suffered from high rates of poverty and severe income inequality. Much of Botswana's economic success is due to its diamond supply and its partnership with the diamond company De Beers. De Beers is a company that has profited from a number of tragedies in Africa, such as apartheid and the civil wars in Angola and Sierra Leone. As mentioned earlier, De Beers was founded by Cecil Rhodes. Botswana owes the majority of its economic success to enriching a company that had already enriched itself through the exploitation of African people.

Here we see that Botswana, despite its apparent economic success, has really operated no different than other neo-colonial governments in post-colonial Africa. Botswana's economic success has been based on its ability to provide diamonds to European owned industries like De Beers, and even then the wealth acquired from the diamonds has not benefited a large segment of the population, especially the San people that have had their rights trampled upon by the Botswana government for the sake of diamond sales.

Another example of the impact of neo-colonialism in Africa is Liberia, a nation which was never politically colonized, although Liberia was economically exploited just the same. Liberia could have been a shining example of Pan-Africanism. This was a nation in Africa that was established by Africans from the United States and the West Indies who had decided to return to their homeland. Ideally, these returning Africans and the native Liberians would work together to build a powerful nation, but this was not to be the case. Not only was Liberia wrecked by the conflict between the returning Africans and the natives, but Liberia was also wrecked by the fact that it was essentially an American colony, though officially Liberia was an independent nation.

In his book *The Condition, Elevation, Emigration, and Destiny of the Colored People of the United States, Politically Considered*, Martin Delany encouraged migration to other parts of the Americas where he felt that African Americans would have more of a chance to prosper, but he was a strict opponent of migration to Liberia. Among the reasons Delany gave for opposing the Liberian colonization scheme was that "it originated in a deep laid scheme of the slaveholders of the country, to *exterminate* the free colored of the American continent; the origin being sufficient to justify us in impugning the motives."

Delany argued that Liberia was not an independent nation, but a nation that was reliant on the slave masters of the United States—in fact, Liberia's capital city, Monrovia, was named after James Monroe, a slave owning president and a supporter of the American Colonization Society. Delany dismissed Liberia by stating: "Liberia in Africa, is a mere dependency of Southern slaveholders, and American Colonizationists, and unworthy of any respectful consideration from us." Delany also compared Liberia to Haiti (Hayti), writing: "What would be thought of the people of Hayti, and their heads of government, if their instructions emanated from the American Anti-Slavery Society, or the British Foreign Missionary Board? Should they be respected at all as a nation? Would they be worthy of it? Certainly not. We do not expect Liberia to be all that Hayti is; but we ask and expect of her, to have a decent respect for herself—to endeavor to be freemen instead of voluntary slaves." Delany showed great foresight because Liberia's continued reliance on American imperialists would hinder Liberia's progress and eventually led to a very bloody civil war.

Liberia has been plagued by the division between the returning African Americans (known as Americo-Liberians) and the natives who suffered many abuses at the hands of the Americo-Liberians. The former American slaves and their descendants who settled in Liberia did not view themselves as Africans who were returning home, although they were welcomed by the Africans of Liberia, who viewed them as long lost kin who had finally returned home. Due to the fact that the Americo-Liberians had been away from Africa for so long, they were culturally more American or Western than they were African, and they had the prejudices of their former slave masters. The Americo-Liberian ruling elite perceived themselves to be superior to the native Liberians. In some cases the natives were even used as slave labor.

One of the best examples of the returning Africans' mentality towards the native Liberians was Edward Wilmot Blyden, one of the great Pan-African intellectuals of his era. Blyden, who was born in Saint Thomas in the Danish West Indies, was under the firm belief that Africans from the United States and the Caribbean should go to Liberia to Christianize the nation and redeem Africa. Blyden also believed that European colonization was a benefit for Africans and took pride in Liberia's connection to Britain. He was a believer in a type of benevolent colonization, which was completely removed from the harsh reality of colonialism in Africa.

Blyden saw Liberia as being "a British Colony in everything but the flag." He boasted that Liberians read "a greater variety of English literature than many an Englishman in England," and Blyden said that Liberia had no desire to "alienate our intellectual allegiance to Great Britain, for that allegiance is a guarantee of political and religious liberty and stimulus to the highest possible human attainment." Blyden also considered it a "great privilege" to speak the language that Shakespeare spoke.

When Blyden was not boasting about how much British culture Liberia was practicing, he was also praising French colonial rule in Africa. He considered it to be a privilege to visit the French Ivory Coast. Blyden "was not only satisfied, but delighted with the results so far of French administration upon the life and prospects of the natives." He confidently felt that "France is doing her part to pacify West Africa, to improve her material condition [...]." Blyden had similar praise of the Germans in Togoland, where he noted that the Germans had built modern European style buildings. Blyden was too optimistic about the role of France, Britain, and Germany in developing Africa. What they were actually doing was exploiting the Africans.

The Americo-Liberians were the ones who held all of the political power, despite being a minority within Liberia's population. This created a type of repressive government in which the rights of the minority group outweighed the rights of the majority. Samuel Doe was the first president of Liberia who was not an Americo-Liberian. Doe forced his way to the presidency by overthrowing and killing the previous president. Doe himself was later overthrown and killed after his tyrannical rule, only to have Liberia fall into the hands of another dictator.

Liberia was established as an independent republic in 1847, but it was not until 1862 that the United States would show any interest in Liberia. This interest was sparked by the discovery of minerals in Liberia, which led many American companies to go to Liberia to mine the gold. America never truly tried to industrialize Liberia, however. Liberia was just seen as a supplier of raw materials, and very often the profits were not equally shared. Between 1904 and 1965, Firestone earned $160 million dollars from Liberian rubber. The Liberian government received only $8 million during that same period. In 1951, Firestone earned three times the amount that the Liberian treasury did, and this was after paying taxes to the Liberian government. Likewise, the Liberian Mining Company also made profits that surpassed the total revenue of the Liberian government.

In Liberia, the United States found a source of rubber that was cheap and totally under their control. In fact, the Liberian ruling class had actually opposed the agreement that Harvey Firestone put forward because they feared that it would undermine their plan for economic development. In the end, American interests beat out the interests of the Liberian ruling class. Firestone was a close friend of Henry Ford. Liberian rubber had turned Akron, Ohio into a powerful center of the rubber tire manufacturing industry, which in turn would aid Ford who had a motor-car industry in Detroit; and as demonstrated above, Liberia was not receiving an equal share in the wealth that was being earned from Liberia's rubber.

President William Tubman of Liberia instituted the "Open Door Policy" to attract foreign investment by offering privileges. The economic terms in Liberia always favored American industry and businesses over that of the Liberian workers, who were frequently abused and mistreated. In 1931 the League of Nations confirmed reports that forced labor and slavery was being used in Liberia. This forced President Charles King, Vice President Allen Yancy, and various other government officials to resign.

Labor leaders were harassed and jailed. When workers went on strike, they were usually brutalized by the state. In 1964 and 1968 there were strikes at Firestone. In response to this, the government sent soldiers and police officers to brutalize the workers. It was not until 1980 that workers in the agricultural sector could even legally organize labor unions.

Not only were workers oppressed in Liberia, but there was very little political freedom. Under Tubman, Liberia became a de facto one-party state where freedom of speech was restricted. Those who spoke out against the government were harassed, imprisoned, and even killed. The repressive nature of the regime in Liberia was such that in 1979, the government ordered security forces to "shoot and kill" Liberians who were participating in a peaceful national demonstration.

America's influence on Liberia also shaped Liberia's foreign policy. President Tubman stood in firm opposition to Kwame Nkrumah and his vision of uniting Africa, and following with the United States' policies of the Cold War, Tubman had no diplomatic ties to the Soviet Union or its satellite countries. President William Tolbert also invited John Vorster, the prime minister of South Africa, to Liberia, which was a direct contradiction to the ban issued by the Organization of African Unity, which prohibited its members from having contact with the apartheid regime of South Africa.

Samuel Doe was also supported by the United States, which backed him while overlooking his brutal dictatorship. During Doe's tenure in office he received $500 million. In return he helped to provide the United States with intelligence on other African states. He played a role in the CIA's operation to support Hissène Habré in overthrowing Goukouni Oueddei and coming to power in Chad. He also played a role in America's attempts to depose Gaddafi in Libya.

American influences also played a role in the Liberian civil wars. The first civil war began in 1989 and was sparked by the rebellion of the National Patriotic Front of Liberia. By the end of the war Samuel Doe had been murdered and Charles Taylor became the president in 1997. Taylor was previously imprisoned in the United States while awaiting extradition to Liberia on charges of corruption. He stated that he escaped from his prison in Massachusetts with the help of the U.S. government, who sent him to overthrow Doe. He was also equipped for his mission by the CIA. Unlike the previous leaders in Liberia, Taylor would prove that he was much harder to control, and he later became an ally to Gaddafi's regime in Libya.

Liberia's problem has been multi-faceted and Liberia's issues are relevant to the neo-colonial influence that the United States has had on Africa. Liberia is a nation partly founded by the interests of American slave holders. The slave holders sent African Americans back to Africa, where the returning African Americans would enslave and oppress the natives in the service of America's economic and political interests. Despite the fact that Liberia was never officially a colony, it has been, in fact, one of the most thoroughly colonized nations in Africa.

Somalia stands out as one of the poorest African nations since achieving its independence. This too is largely a result of European colonization in East Africa, which has created a number of problems for Somalis in the region. In a sense, Somalia had an advantage over other African nations, given that, as Martin Meredith writes, "Somalis possessed a common language and a common culture based on pastoral customs and traditions." Unlike other African nations, Somalia was more culturally homogenous, but this also worked to Somalia's disadvantage. This strong sense of nationalism led some Somalis to fight for the unification of the Somali people. This goal was complicated by the borders that were drawn up in East Africa.

During the colonial period, Somalia was divided between Britain, Italy, France, and Ethiopia. In 1944, before the end of World War II, the British proposed uniting all of the Somali people into a single nation. This was to include Ogaden (the Somali territory that was under Ethiopian rule), Italian Somaliland, and French Somaliland (which later became Djibouti). The British plan neglected the Somalis living in the British colony of Kenya. The United States objected to including Ogaden in Somaliland because Ethiopia was an ally of the United Nations. Italian Somaliland and British Somaliland were then merged into the independent nation of Somalia in 1960.

In 1963, a secessionist movement in Kenya which was supported by Somalia emerged. Many Somalis wanted to unite all Somali people into a larger Somali nation, but this was opposed by the Kenyan government. This led to the Shifta War, which lasted from 1963 until 1968. This conflict was in part the continuing legacy of the divide and rule tactics that was used by the British colonial authorities in Kenya. Under British rule, Somalis were considered to be a distinct group from the rest of the population in Kenya.

The Devastation and Economics of the African Holocaust

The Northern Frontier Province region, where Somalis lived, was largely neglected by the British administration. This was one of the reasons why the Somalis continued to associate more with Somalis outside of Kenya than they did with the other Kenyans. This pattern of neglect continued after independence and Somalis continued to associate more with Somalia than with their native Kenya. These Kenyan born Somalis were very sympathetic with the Pan-Somali ideology that emerged in the 1950s. By 1962, more than 87% of Somalis living in Kenya expressed a desire to unite with the Somali Republic. A Somali political party known as the Northern Province Peoples' Progressive Party (NPPPP) openly objected to being included in the Kenyan government. The British ignored this, however. When Kenya became independent in 1963, the Somali region was included. Mathilde Simon describes this move on the part of Britain as follows:

> By handing the Northern province to Kenyan nationalists, colonial powers handed the role of the oppressor to Kenya, who then clearly reinforced this oppressive role by using a level of violence that was not proportional, in an attempt to control the threat. The fight for self-determination became the fight against the Kenyan government.

Shortly after Kenya gained independence, a number of Somalis began their own struggle for independence from Kenya. Somalis took up arms and began attacks on police stations and polling places. These raiders were eventually labeled *shifta* by the Kenyan government. The word "shifta" means bandit. This term had political implications for both sides of the war. The Kenyan government used it to depict the Somalis that were fighting for independence as bandits and criminals. The Somalis embraced the term as one that referred to a sort of romantic criminal who raided and plundered for their people.

As the war waged on, the Kenyan government found itself in a difficult situation. The tactics that they used to defeat the shifta had failed. They were also at the brink of war with Somalia, which was assisting the shifta movement. Kenya's options were also limited, as the government did not have the funding necessary for a war with the shifta. The war was very costly due to the usage of landmines by the shifta. This proved especially costly to the Kenyan government, which relied on motor vehicle transport and did not have effective counter-mine capabilities. Unable to defeat the shifta militarily, the Kenyan government had to defeat them politically.

The British had predicted that due to the cost of the war Kenya would simply agree to allow the Somalis to secede from Kenya, but the Kenyan government declared that "Kenya will not allow any part of its territory to be dismembered and will defend her territorial integrity by every means." The problem that Kenya was facing was common in post-colonial Africa. A number of African nations found themselves fighting wars to maintain the borders that were drawn up by the colonialists. The civil war in Nigeria was fought over attempts by the Igbo people to create a separate republic of their own. Eritrea fought a decades long war to obtain its independence from Ethiopia. After two civil wars the South Sudan became a separate nation of its own after seceding from the north.

Waning support for the war caused Somalia to reconcile with Kenya. The Somali government stopped supporting the shifta in Kenya. This essentially ended any hopes for secession among the Kenyan Somalis. The shifta continued their raids, despite no longer having the support of Somalia and the Kenyan Somali citizens behind them. The shifta also began turning against their own, including killing and mutilating Somali elders that were sent to negotiate an end to the raids. In the long-run, the shifta revealed themselves to merely be the bandits that the Kenyan government had presented them as, rather than being patriotic freedom fighters.

The end of the Shifta War was not the end of the ethnic struggles in Kenya. Somalis were marginalized by the Kenyan government. This included gross human rights violations such as the massacre at Garissa, in which the Kenyan military killed 3,000 Somalis. Garissa would later be the location of another massacre when, on April 2, 2015, al-Shabaab attacked Garissa University College, killing 147 people and injuring many more.

American relations with Somalia following independence in 1960 was largely shaped by Somalia's strategic location, being next to the Red Sea and the Persian Gulf. These relations cooled when Mohammed Siad Barre came to power in October 1969, after staging a coup. Barre was a proponent of both scientific socialism and Somali nationalism. His goal was to unite all Somali people under one flag. This obviously was a difficult task, given that Somalis were also living in neighboring African nations. This made Barre's relationship with those nations strained, especially with Ethiopia. Barre's support of socialism also made Somalia a key player in the Cold War. The Soviet Union provided arms to Barre to attack Ethiopia, which was America's main ally in the region.

America's policy in east Africa changed in 1975. In Ethiopia, Haile Selassie was overthrown by a Marxist pro-Soviet government known as DERGUE, which was led by Mengistu Haile Mariam. Under Selassie, Ethiopia was an American ally in the region, but Mariam's pro-Soviet position changed America's relationship with Ethiopia. Barre, who was previously pro-Soviet, found his relationship with the Soviet Union becoming strained. The Soviet Union attempted to reconcile Ethiopia and Somalia, but Barre's Marxism came secondary to his Somali nationalism. For these reasons, America's relationship with Somalia improved.

The United States increased both military and economic assistance to Somalia. It is estimated that throughout the 1980s, the Barre regime was given $800 million of aid. The Barre regime became dependent on this foreign aid, including food aid. Somalia, which had been self-sufficient with food grains, now became dependent on imported food. Of course, such food aid mostly benefited the ruling elite. Throughout the 1980s, Barre's regime became more repressive and corrupt. Human rights groups criticized America's support of such a repressive government, but the relationship between Barre and America would last as long as it served America's interests. By 1989, Congress managed to successfully cut off military assistance to Somalia, but humanitarian and economic assistance would continue.

By the mid-1980s Somalia was wrecked by civil war as other clans armed themselves to overthrow Siad Barre's unpopular regime and, by 1990, Barre had lost most of the country and was desperately holding on to Mogadishu. To make matters worse for Barre, America lost use for him. America was able to set up a base of operations in Saudi Arabia and no longer needed Barre as a strategic ally in the region. Without the American assistance Barre was finally driven out of office in 1991. Somalia fell into a state of chaos, as rival clans fought each other for control over the nation. By 1992, Somalia had no central government. The country was torn apart by rival warlords fighting over control of the nation. Mohamed Farrah Aidid would emerge as the most powerful of these warlords.

The civil war in Somalia was complicated by the fact that historically Somalis were never collectively governed by a unified central government structure. Somalis were organized into clans. These clans often warred with each other whenever disputes emerged. This was a problem for the British because after they created the borders in the region the Somali clans often fought cross-border conflicts. To protect their interests, the British attempted to restrict Somali migration into Kenya from Ethiopia and Italian Somaliland. These attempts failed, however, as Somalis, a traditionally nomadic people, continued to migrate across borders.

The fighting in Somalia created a humanitarian disaster. A large number of Somalis were starving to death. The United Nations responded by sending a relief effort. The distribution of food proved to be a difficult task since Somali warlords often seized these food shipments to feed their own soldiers. President George Bush ordered that the American military be used to deliver humanitarian relief into Somalia. This operation had successfully reduced the number of deaths from starvation in Somalia. One of the conditions that Bush laid out for American involvement in this mission was that the UN would take control of the operation within six months.

The UN took control of the operation in May 1993. Problems began to arise, however. In 1993, over twenty Pakistani peacekeeping troops were killed by Somalis. Aidid was blamed for this incident and there was an effort put forward to secure Aidid's arrest. Admiral Jonathan Howe was especially determined to capture Aidid.

These attempts to capture Aidid only made the foreign presence in Somalia even more unpopular. In July, American commanders received information that Aidid was planning to attend a meeting at the house of an associate named Abdi Hassan Qaybdiid. American commanders launched an airstrike. Cobra helicopters descended on the building and blew it to pieces. Fifty-four people were killed in this strike, although Somali sources listed as many as seventy-three casualties. A 90 year old elder was among the dead, but Aidid was not inside the house.

Howe was satisfied with this strike, although other officials were horrified that the UN was involved in this massacre. Ann Wright, an American lawyer, resigned from her post as the head of the United Nations Operation in Somalia's (UNOSOM) justice division in protest. She also wrote: "Unosom should anticipate that some organizations and member states will characterize a deliberate attack meant to kill the occupants without giving all the building occupants a chance to surrender as nothing less than murder committed in the name of the United Nations."

This assault was not the only instance of outright murder being committed on the part of the UN. One of the most controversial moments of the UN's involvement in Somalia at the time was what became known as the "Somalia Affair" in 1993. During this incident, a sixteen year old Somali boy named Shidane Arone was beaten to death by members of the Canadian Airborne Regiment, which had been sent to Somalia by Canada as part of the UN's peacekeeping mission. Arone not only endured repeated blows to the head, but burning and suffocation as well. The UN had initially helped to alleviate the food crisis in Somalia, but they had overstayed their welcome in the eyes of the Somalis, who began to refer to the UN headquarters as the "camp of the murderers."

Howe was unrelenting in his desire to capture Aidid. He requested reinforcements from the American special forces. A team of Rangers and a Delta Force squad was dispatched to Mogadishu for the purpose of capturing Aidid. The mission was met with difficulties from the start, as the American forces often found themselves storming into buildings and arresting the wrong people.

They finally found an opportunity to apprehend two of Aidid's closest associates, who were having a meeting nearby the Bakara Market of the Black Sea district in Mogadishu. This mission would be a difficult one, given that they were plotting a raid in Aidid's stronghold. They encountered problems in the mission when two Black Hawk helicopters were shot down by the Somalis. Rescue convoys attempted to rescue the downed helicopters, but they struggled to make it through the gunfire and barricades.

In the end the mission was a failure that resulted in the deaths of 18 soldiers and more than 70 more being wounded. The corpses of two of the dead soldiers were dragged around the streets by angry mobs for the world to see. The Somalis viewed this battle as a victory, having successfully forced the Americans to retreat. This battle became known to them as *Malinti Rangers* or "The Day of the Rangers." Although Somalis celebrated this battle as a victory, as many as a thousand Somalis were killed. Many of them were civilians who were caught in the crossfire. In response to this catastrophe, President Bill Clinton called off the hunt for Aidid and withdrew American involvement in Somalia. Clinton also blamed the UN for the deaths of the American soldiers, although the UN had nothing to do with the operation.

The victory for the Somalis was only a symbolic one, however. The civil wars in Somalia continued. The retreat of America from Somalia was followed by a withdrawal of international aid groups. Somalia was also once again faced with starvation. After spending $4 billion in an attempt to rebuild Somalia, the UN was forced to retreat.

In 2006 the Islamic Courts Union (ICU) took control over large parts of Somalia. The ICU managed to bring some semblance of law and order to a nation that had endured decades of internal conflicts. The ICU set up schools and oversaw local disputes. They also approved transactions such as buying houses and cars, and oversaw weddings and divorces. Moreover, they were able to reduce violence in the areas that were under their control.

There were problems within the ICU, however, as the factions did not share the same interpretations of Sharia law. The al-Shabaab group was especially known for their repressive practices, which included stoning a 13 year old girl to death for committing adultery because she was raped. Suspected homosexuals were also stoned by al-Shabaab. The repressive practices of al-Shabaab were in contrast to the general movement towards the reformation of Islamic law in Somalia. For instance, in 1975 the passage of a Family Law allowed women equal right to inherit property.

Moreover, the ICU was not internationally recognized as a governing body in Somalia. In 2004, a regional body that consisted of Uganda, Kenya, Ethiopia, Sudan, Eritrea, Djibouti, and Somalia established what was called the Transitional Federal Government (TFG) to restore order in Somalia. This led to the creation of the Transitional Federal Institutions (TFI) in Somalia, of which Abdullahi Yusuf Ahmed served as president. It was the TFG that was internationally recognized as Somalia's government. The TFG and the ICU clashed over control of Somalia. TFG was backed by Ethiopia, the United States, and the African Union.

The ICU became a concern for the United States in the wake of the 9/11 attacks that destroyed the Twin Towers and killed nearly 3,000 Americans. Following these attacks President George W. Bush initiated the "War on Terror." Ethiopia became a strategic location in East Africa to carry out this agenda because of its proximity to Somalia. America feared that Somalia would become a haven for terrorists. Despite having a transitional government in power, the ICU remained in control of much of the nation. Yusuf Ahmed resigned in 2008, acknowledging that he had failed to unite the country.

Ethiopia had a troubled history with Somalia which even predates Somalia's independence. Under the rule of Emperor Menelik II, parts of Somalia were conquered by Ethiopia. This territory was retained by Ethiopia when Somalia became an independent nation. As mentioned before, many Somalis wanted a unified Somali state which was to include even those Somalis living outside of Somalia. This led to a number of clashes between Ethiopia and Somalia over the regions of Ethiopia where Somalis lived. This included an armed conflict between the two nations in February 1964. There was also the Ogaden War, which lasted from 1977 to 1978. Prior to Ethiopia's 2006 invasion of Somalia, there was already a history of warfare and animosity between the two nations.

In November 2006, the Ethiopian parliament voted to pass a resolution which allowed the government to "take all necessary steps to ward off attacks by the Islamic Council in Somalia." Ethiopia then invaded Somalia. Initially Ethiopia only planned to stay in Somalia for a few weeks, but the war stretched on for two years. By the end of the war Mogadishu had come under Ethiopian control. It was not until January 2008 that President Yusuf Ahmed set foot in Mogadishu. The war was initially a success for Ethiopia in that they managed to break the strength of the ICU and help to install a government that they felt was more favorable for them, although Somalia remained disunited.

The Ethiopian invasion of Somalia was supported by America, which provided both military and economic assistance. The military assistance consisted of both military advisors and weapons. One Ethiopian journalist declared: "The mercenary Meles Zenawi was willing to offer Ethiopian forces to carry out Washington's agenda for Somalia. The end justifies the means, especially when it is Ethiopian lives that have to be sacrificed." This comment speaks to the unpopularity of the Zenawi government among many Ethiopians who accused the government of corruption and the abuse of state power. This has included harassing and jailing journalists. The Bush administration failed to condemn the Ethiopian government for such abuses while they were offering support for Ethiopia to invade Somalia.

The Ethiopian troops finally pulled out of Somalia in January 2009. The result of this war was that it created far more problems than it solved. With the collapse of the ICU, al-Shabaab remained and continued the fight against Ethiopia. Valter Vilkko wrote that al-Shabaab "was widely seen as a defender of Somali interests against the Ethiopian invaders. The ICU had been able to bring order and security, which led many to hope that al Shabaab, regardless of means and ideology, could do the same." The Ethiopian government, which was enduring issues of its own such as a drought, made what turned out to be a disastrous move in interfering with the politics of a neighboring country. Napoleon A. Bamfo described the invasion as thus:

> Ethiopia's invasion seems an unmitigated waste and one can only hope that African governments would learn a lesson from it before any flippantly decides to copy Ethiopia's example to invade its neighbor.

The borders that were drawn by Europeans during the scramble for Africa would have a profound impact on Africa long after independence. Perhaps nowhere was this truer than Somalia. After Somalia gained its independence it became a nation of rival clans that was ruled by a dictatorial and murderous central government. Many Somalis found themselves living outside of Somalia, which created a number of issues as well. Moreover, Somalia's situation was complicated by an American foreign policy in the region, which, with few exceptions, has helped to create more chaos and instability in the region than it has actually solved. Somalia's poverty and suffering is yet another example of how European colonization disrupted the political and economic development of African societies.

Julius Nyerere expressed the sum total of the colonial experience of African people in the Arusha Declaration, stating: "We have been oppressed a great deal, we have been exploited a great deal and we have been disregarded a great deal. Now we want a revolution—a revolution which brings an end to our weakness, so that we are never again exploited, oppressed, or humiliated." This is a profound statement which speaks to the level of exploitation that African people have experienced throughout the years. Nyerere's call for a revolution is also profound because it recognizes that a fundamental change in the system is required, and one which will end the weakness of African people that has allowed them to collectively be oppressed.

The justifications of slavery and colonization were that they were benefits to African people, but it has been demonstrated that this was not the case at all. Africans suffered in a number of inhumane ways. The sum total of European's interaction with Africa has been one largely of economic exploitation, which has enriched European people and has left African people in a state of poverty and suffering.

References:

Adam Hochschild, *King Leopold's Ghost*, (New York: Mariner Books, 1998).

Alison Redmayne, "Mkwawa and the Hehe Wars," *The Journal of African History*, Vol. 9, No. 3 (1968), pp. 409-436

Ameila Cook and Jeremy Sarkin, "Is Botswana the Miracle of Africa? Democracy, the Rule of Law, and Human Rights Versus Economic Development," *Transnational Law & Contemporary Problems* Vol. 19, Spring 2010.

Bill Brummel (producer), *Blood Diamonds*, 2006.

CL.R. James, *A History of Pan-African Revolt*, (PM Press, 2012).

Collin Palmer, *Eric Williams and the Making of the Modern Caribbean*, (The University of North Carolina Press, 2008).

Commander George Shorey, "Bystander Non-Intervention and the Somalia Incident," *Canadian Military Journal*, 2000-2001.

Edward Wilmot Blyden, *West Africa Before Europe*, 1905.

Eugenia W. Herbert, "Smallpox Inoculation in Africa," *The Journal of African History*, Vol. 16, No. 4 (1975), pp. 539-559

Frank Chalk, "Du Bois and Garvey Confront Liberia: Two Incidents of the Coolidge Years" *Canadian Journal of African Studies/Revue Canadienne des Études Africaines,* Vol. 1, No. 2 (Nov., 1967), pp. 135-142

George Klay Kieh Jr., Policy and the First Liberian Civil War," *The Journal of Pan African Studies*, vol.5, no.1, March 2012.

Herman J. Cohen, "Somalia and the United States: A Long and Troubled History," *All Africa*, January 21, 2002.

H.R. Fox Bourne, "The Uganda Protectorate and Its Relation to the Sudan," *The Imperial and Asiatic Quarterly Review and Colonial Record*, Third Series, Volume III, January-April 1899.

Ian Cobain and Richard Norton-Taylor, "Sins of colonialists lay concealed for decades in secret archive," *The Guardian*, April 18th 2012.

Ian Cobain, Richard Norton-Taylor, and Clar Ni Chonghaile, "Mau Mau veterans win right to sue British government," *The Guardian*, October 5th, 2012.

James Frederick Cunningham, *Uganda and Its People*, 1905.

Joseph Casely Hayford, *Gold Coast Native Institutions: With Thoughts Upon a Healthy Imperial Policy for the Gold Coast and Ashanti*, (London: Sweet and Maxwell, Limited, 1903).

Julius Nyerere, "Africa: The Third Liberation," address given at the University of Edinburgh, Scotland, on October 9, 1997 as part of Scotland-Africa 97.

Kemi Rotimi, "Jaja and Nana in the Niger Delta Region of Nigeria: Proto-Nationalists or Emergent Capitalists," *The Journal of Pan African Studies*, vol.2, no.7, December 2008.

Kwame Nkrumah, *Africa Must Unite*, (Frederick A. Praeger, 1963).

Lieutenant-Commander George Shorey, "Bystander Non-Intervention and the Somalia Incident," *Canadian Military Journal*, Winter 2000-2001, pg. 19-28

Major John Ringquist, "Bandit or Patriot: The Kenyan Shifta War 1963-1968," *Baltic Security and Defence Review*, volume 13, issue

1, 2011.

Martin Delany, *The Condition, Elevation, Emigration, and Destiny of the Colored People of the United States*, 1852.

Martin Meredith, *The Fate of Africa*, (Public Affairs, 2011).

Marvin Perry, Joseph R. Penden, Theodore H. Von Laue, George W. Bock (editors), *Sources of the Western Tradition: Volume II: From the Renaissance to the Present*, (Wadsworth, Cengage Learning, 2008).

Mary Kingsley, *West African Studies* (London: The Macmillan Company, 1899).

Mathilde Simon, "The April 2015 Attack in Garissa by al Shabaab," *Foreign Policy Journal*, June 12, 2015.

Napoleon A. Bamfo, "Ethiopia's invasion of Somalia in 2006: Motives and lessons learned," *African Journal of Political Science and International Relations* Vol. 4(2), pp. 055-065, February 2010.

Ngũgĩ wa Thiong'o, *Something Torn and Something New: An African Renaissance*, (BasicCivitas Books, 2009).

Ray Logan, "The Historical Aspects of Pan-Africanism A Personal Chronicle," African Forum, 1965.

Robert Pickering Ashe, *Chronicles of Uganda*

Shana Willis, "Jonas Savimbi: Washington's 'Freedom Fighter,' Africa's 'Terrorist,'" *Foreign Policy in Focus*, February 1, 2002.

Thomas Collelo (editor), *Angola: A Country Study*. Washington: GPO for the Library of Congress, 1991.

___*Chad: A Country Study*. Washington: GPO for the Library of Congress, 1988.

Toyin Falola, *Colonialism and Violence in Nigeria*, (Indiana University Press, 2009).

George Klay Kieh, Jr., "Neo-Colonialism: American Foreign Policy and the First Liberian Civil War," *The Journal of Pan African Studies*, vol.5, no.1, March 2012

Walter Rodney, *How Europe Underdeveloped Africa*, (Bogle-L'Ouverture Publications, 1972).

Winston McGowan, "Fula Resistance to French Expansion into Futa Jallon 1889-1896," *The Journal of African History*, Vol. 22, No. 2 (1981), pp. 245-26

More Books by the Author

Malcolm X, Bob Marley, and Other Essays
One Caribbean and Other Essays
Yekola Lingala (Learn Lingala)
The Life, Goals, and Achievements of Marcus Garvey
Jumbie Tales
Poetry & Wisdom
Kingdoms and Civilizations of Africa

www.ingramcontent.com/pod-product-compliance
Lightning Source LLC
Chambersburg PA
CBHW071207280526
45787CB00002B/596